GAYLORD

Women Inventors
& Their Discoveries

Women Inventors
& Their Discoveries

Ethlie Ann Vare and Greg Ptacek

Foreword by Ruth Handler

illustrated with photographs

The Oliver Press, Inc.,
Minneapolis

The Oliver Press
Josiah King House
2709 Lyndale Avenue South
Minneapolis, MN 55408

Library of Congress Cataloging-in-Publication Data

Vare, Ethlie Ann.
Women inventors and their discoveries / Ethlie Ann Vare and
Greg Ptacek ; foreword by Ruth Handler.

p.   cm. — (Profiles)
Includes bibliographical references and index.
    Summary: Surveys the lives and work of such innovative
women as Grace Hopper, Fannie Farmer, C. J. Walker, and
Stephanie Kwolek.
ISBN 1-881508-06-4 : $14.95
1. Women inventors—United Sates—Biography—Juvenile litera-
ture. 2. Inventions—United States—History—Juvenile literature.
[1. Women inventors. 2. Inventors.]   I. Ptacek, Greg.
II. Title. III. Series: Profiles (Minneapolis, Minn.)
T39.V37   1993   92-38268
609.2'273—dc20   CIP
[B]   AC

ISBN 1-881508-06-4
Profiles VII
Printed in the United States of America

99 98 97 96 95 94 93   8 7 6 5 4 3 2 1

Contents

Foreword

*Y*ou don't have to be an engineer or a mathematician or a scientist to be an inventor. To be an inventor, you have to have certain creative talents: the talent to observe and the talent to conceive of a new idea. You have to be able to see a need, and you have to have a specific, concrete understanding of how to fill that need.

You can hire technicians and manufacturers to bring your idea to fruition. You don't have to know what materials will be used or what the manufacturing process will be. But you cannot go to these people and say to them, "Let's do this better." You have to know exactly what you want.

My first successful creations, Barbie and Ken, came from observing my own daughter playing with paper dolls. She always chose grown-up dolls, and I realized she was using the doll to project her own dreams of her future. I was convinced that if I could turn this play pattern with paper dolls into a three-dimensional doll, I could fill a very real need in the life of little girls.

My next noteworthy creation was the Nearly Me breast prosthesis. This came from my personal experience of having to wear an artificial breast after my mastectomy. I was determined to design and market a totally new type of artificial breast—one that looked and felt natural and was sold by clerks who were trained to be sensitive and helpful.

With all my creations, I have observed a need—a big, fat hole in the market—and insisted that my product be better than anything else in its field. And in all cases, the characteristics of the product had to be completely and carefully defined by the creator, the person with the idea.

I don't personally hold a patent on Barbie, but I am the inventor of the Barbie doll. Not everybody can be an inventor or a designer or a creator. You have to be blessed with certain creative talents. Do you have the talents of an inventor?

Ruth Handler

Introduction

"Women don't invent," says conventional wisdom, and any facts inconveniently to the contrary somehow slip between the cracks of history. But women have been inventing throughout history. From Hypatia of Alexandria, who invented some of the first laboratory instruments, to Marie Curie, who began the Atomic Age, women have been discovering, inventing, and creating.

Why have so few women been recognized for the products of their imaginations? Some did not want recognition. Take Catherine Littlefield Greene, for example, whom some people believe invented the cotton gin. A Revolutionary War hero's genteel widow, she would have considered herself unladylike to engage in "trade." So, she let Eli Whitney file the patent. On the other hand, Dr. Lise Meitner was demoted in her absence by her associate Dr. Otto Hahn to the status of "coworker" when, in fact, she was *coinventor* of nuclear fission. Moreover, she coined the term! In her own time, Lady Mary Wortley Montagu was recognized for introducing smallpox inoculation to the Western world. But when Edward Jenner reintroduced the concept 50 years later, history gave him all the glory.

But there have also been some women, like the women in this book, who became millionaires and won international acclaim because of their innovations. Barbara McClintock won the Nobel Prize in 1983 for her discoveries; Ruth Handler became president of Mattel, a multinational corporation; Madam C. J. Walker, the daughter of former slaves, became the first black woman millionaire in the United States; and Stephanie Kwolek was the first woman nominated to the Inventors Hall of Fame.

They beat the odds. Bringing an idea to fruition is remarkable in the first place. These women did it in the face of entrenched gender prejudice and, often, great personal adversity: Elizabeth Lucas Pinckney lost an infant child; Martha Coston was widowed at 21; Fannie Merritt Farmer was stricken with polio at 16; Sarah Walker was orphaned at 7. And both Stephanie Kwolek and Sara Josephine Baker were very young when their fathers died.

They say that which doesn't kill you makes you stronger and that necessity is the mother of invention. Meet some very strong, very inventive, and very feisty women.

While no picture of Elizabeth Lucas Pinckney is known to exist, she might have resembled her daughter, Harriott Pinckney Horry.

1

Elizabeth Lucas Pinckney

*E*lizabeth Lucas Pinckney—known as Eliza—grew up in an environment very much like that of Scarlett O'Hara in *Gone with the Wind.* She lived in a big mansion on a southern plantation, where young women of her class rarely left the house and instead were expected to while away the hours planning parties and managing servants. So probably no one was more surprised than Eliza when, at age 17, she was put in complete charge of a 600-acre plantation and a 1500-acre property in South Carolina and made responsible for an ailing mother, a younger sister, 20 slaves, and an assortment of employees.

In 1739, Britain and Spain were at war, and Eliza's father, a lieutenant colonel in the British army, was forced to return to his military post in Antigua. With no one else in his family able to take over the plantation, but with confidence in his oldest daughter's abilities, he went to war, leaving her to manage everything.

Eliza proved to be no ordinary 17 year old. Instead of being overwhelmed, she dove right in and applied herself to the job. Two years later, she became responsible for the development of a commercial crop, indigo, that enriched the economy of South Carolina and made her a wealthy woman by the time she was 21.

The oldest of four children, Eliza was born in 1722 in the West Indies, where she spent her early years. Later her family sent her to England to complete her education. When she was 16, her father, George Lucas, brought the family to Wappoo Creek, a plantation he had inherited in South Carolina, because he hoped the climate would improve his wife's health.

According to Eliza's letter book, during that first year she read extensively (as she always had), played her flute, practiced her French, and tutored her sister, Polly. She even taught reading to a pair of young black children whom she hoped to make "school mistresses for the rest of the Negro children," if her father approved.

"I have a little library well furnished," she recorded in her notebook, "for my papa has left me most of his books." To the surprise of some of her older visitors, Eliza quoted Milton, and her lively intellect prompted her to read with great interest such writers as John

Locke, Virgil, Plutarch, and the legal authority, Thomas Wood.

The plantation was some 17 miles from Charleston by land and 6 miles by water, and Eliza enjoyed brief visits in society there. Her observations, recorded in a letter book that is one of the largest surviving collections of letters of a colonial lady, reveal that she could write with originality and charm. But largely she gave her considerable energies to the plantation routine, a practice that served her well when events overtook her.

We know little about the extent of her formal education, although much has been recorded about the accomplishments of her sons, both of whom were well educated. However, reflecting the custom of the times—that education for women was selective—even less information is available about how much schooling her daughter, Harriott, received.

It was a year later when her father left for Antigua and Eliza took over. She wrote to a friend that the task was hard. "It requires . . . more business and fatigue than you can imagine." Still, the challenge proved to be opportunity in disguise.

At her father's urging, Eliza began to experiment with new crops suitable for upland cultivation and export, such as ginger, cotton, and alfalfa. But after much trial and error, her greatest success was with indigo, which she succeeded in growing successfully from seeds her father sent her from the West Indies. This success was a remarkable achievement considering that a plantation owner had tried and discarded a crop of indigo near Charleston 70 years earlier. No one in the entire country had been able to grow it successfully between then and Eliza's triumphant attempt.

What was so important about growing indigo domestically? Why was Eliza's indigo important, and what made it become a mainstay of the economy of South Carolina and the colonies for three decades until the Revolutionary War intervened?

Indigo is a dyestuff used in printing inks and for vat dying of cotton. It was known in India and Egypt as long ago as 1600 B.C., and archaeologists have discovered mummies wrapped in indigo-dyed cloth. For commercial use, it is prepared in the form of dye cakes, and its chief attribute is that it adds a strong blue color of great permanence. During Eliza's time, English cloth manufacturers valued it greatly and grudgingly bought what they needed from France, the only source available to them.

Eliza was more than a dedicated agriculturist. She was also a good businesswoman. She reasoned that if a fine grade of blue dye cakes from indigo grown in South Carolina could be prepared for cloth manufacturers in England, two important problems would be solved at the same time: the British would no longer have to buy indigo from the French, and South Carolina would have a new product to sell. That was important because the

The indigo plant from which dyes were made

war had sharply diminished the European demand for the South's staple product, rice. But, she admitted, "I was ignorant both of the proper season for sowing it and the soil best adapted to it."

She wrote in her journal in 1739 that she "had greater hopes from the indigo . . . than any of the rest of the things I had tryd," providing she could have the seed from the West Indies earlier the following year. Her hopes were well warranted, but success didn't come overnight, and there were setbacks.

Consider just one of the problems. Converting the plant from which indigo is derived involves a process in which the plant is allowed to soften and ferment in vats of water. When the colorless form of indigo emerges in the mix, stirring it causes the indigo to oxidize and turn blue—the blue so highly prized by manufacturers of cotton and ink.

To help in developing the procedure, Eliza's father sent her an experienced dye maker who came from the British island of Montserrat. She looked forward to his arrival with high anticipation, because it was a step that promised to confirm that the seeds provided her would produce the dye they were looking for. Instead, in the best tradition of a dime novel mystery, he turned out to be a scoundrel! Rather than helping, he created a disaster. Fearful that competition from South Carolina would ruin the indigo trade of his own island, he deliberately added something to the mix, changing the color of the indigo so it was spoiled.

Undiscouraged, Eliza continued her experiments, this time with the help of Patrick Cromwell, a second professional dye maker sent by her father. When, finally, in 1744, six pounds of a successful crop were sent to England and found "better than the French indigo," she elatedly distributed seeds from that crop to a great many planters who soon were growing and profiting from the new export product. A new industry was born, and Eliza Pinckney had created it! Two years later, South

Carolina shipped 40,0000 pounds of indigo to England, followed by 100,000 pounds the year after.

The French, who long enjoyed a monopoly on the sale of indigo, had been cavalier about the threat of competition from the American colonies. Now they made the exportation of the plants and seeds used to make indigo a capital crime, but it was too late. Eliza Pinckney's indigo provided all that the colonies needed for themselves and for export.

By this time, Eliza was 21. She was successful, rich, and independent and had turned down two marriage proposals. She chose to marry Charles Pinckney, a highly respected lawyer from Charleston, a childless widower. At one point, he was Speaker of the Commons House of Assembly and later a senator. Charles and his first wife had been close friends of Eliza, and he had often lent her books.

For his bride, Charles built a handsome house on Charleston's waterfront. At his plantation, Eliza continued to experiment, cultivating flax and hemp. She even initiated the culture of silkworms and established a private enterprise for the manufacture of silk.

At the birth of the first of her four children, Eliza wrote her new goals: "To be a good mother to my children . . . to instill piety, virtue, and true religion into them; to correct their errors whatever uneasiness it may give myself."

For 14 years, the Pinckneys lived happily, spending

Charleston's waterfront at the time Elizabeth Lucas Pinckney was a young woman

much of their time in London, the last 5 of those years after he was appointed commissioner for the colony. Their intention was to live there until their children finished their education. But when war with France broke out, they returned to South Carolina, leaving their two boys at school. Tragically, on a return trip from England, Charles contracted malaria and died. Eliza, now in her middle 30s, was once again a plantation manager.

One of Eliza's four children died in infancy, but she had reason to be proud of the accomplishments of the others. Despite their long years in England, sons Charles and Thomas were devoted to the American cause and returned to Charleston before the outbreak of

the Revolution. Both became heroes in that war, serving their country with distinction.

When Pinckney was asked how her sons felt about the question of Colony versus King, she reportedly gave "no advice and attempted no influence, for having done her best while they were boys to make them wise and good men, she now thankfully acknowledged that they surpassed her in wisdom as in stature."

Her son Charles served as Washington's aide in 1777. After the war, he represented South Carolina at the Constitutional Convention, served on a special mission to France, and was the candidate for the Federalist party for president in 1804 and 1808.

Thomas was governor of the state in 1787 and later minister to Great Britain and special commissioner to Spain. He negotiated with Spain the very important

Charles Cotesworth Pinckney (1746-1825) served his state and his country as both a military and a political leader.

Pinckney Treaty that allowed the colonies use of the Mississippi River.

Both men continued their mother's tradition of experimental agriculture. Ironically, Charles was one of the first planters to grow long-staple cotton, the crop that ultimately replaced indigo as the economic bulwark of the South.

During the later years of her life, Eliza spent much time at the plantation of her widowed daughter, Harriott Horry, surrounded by grandchildren, including the three daughters of her son Charles, whose wife had died. On May 26, 1793, in Philadelphia, Elizabeth "Eliza" Pinckney died of cancer. She was so highly regarded for her contribution to the country's growth and economic well being, that President George Washington, at his own request, was a pallbearer at her funeral.

Pinckney's accomplishments were not the result of individual, special talents. Rather, they reflected her genuine interest and curiosity about the world around

Thomas Pinckney (1750-1828) rose to the rank of major general in the War of 1812.

At Hampton Plantation, their South Carolina home after the American Revolution, Harriott Pinckney Horry and her mother received George Washington.

her and her willingness to explore possibilities. She looked upon the challenges with which her father presented her not as burdens, but as opportunities. She dealt with them successfully because she was supported by the confidence her father demonstrated in her ability to make decisions. Despite the distance between them during the war and her remarkable success, Eliza continued to welcome his advice. His appointment as lieutenant governor of the island colony of Antigua in 1738 attested to his abilities as a government official, but the confidence he showed in his daughter attested to his wisdom as a father.

Natural indigo as a major product of the South was

Cotton ultimately replaced indigo as South Carolina's leading crop and became the most important product of the South's slave-based economy.

replaced by cotton after the Revolution of 1776, and synthetic indigo has since replaced natural indigo. But for its time as a profitable crop, it was South Carolina's key to financial stability for 30 years, and thanks to Elizabeth Lucas Pinckney it helped establish an economic base for the young nation of former British colonies.

Naval authorities in the nineteenth century had difficulty accepting Martha Coston's role in the development of such an important wartime device as the signal flare.

2

Martha Coston

*T*he pistols that sailors use to send flares into the sky, warning other ships of dangers or signaling to one another the conditions of the sea, are called "Very Pistols," after the naval officer who perfected the firing mechanism. But the flares themselves—and the idea behind them—were the invention of a doomed young man named Benjamin Coston. And they were developed, manufactured, and marketed by Martha Coston, his penniless widow, who labored for years out of love and sheer desperation.

In the Civil War, these vital communication devices were known as Coston Night Signals. And it was to Martha's everlasting annoyance that the United States Navy stole her thunder and her credit simply because she was a woman. At least Martha Coston made sure that no one ever stole the royalties she eventually earned!

Early on, Martha Hunt, called "Mattie" by her family and "Pattie" by her friends, displayed the stubborn strength that marked her life and career. Born in Baltimore in 1826, she moved to Philadelphia when she was 4. At 14, she fell in love. That event changed her life. Years later, she described how it happened in her autobiography, *A Signal Success:*

One beautiful summer day, during the school vacation, I went to a picnic with my schoolmate and particular friend, Nellie Foster. An unusual excitement took possession of me. I remember now how my fingers trembled as I tied back my willful curls with a piece of soft, blue ribbon, though I did not fail to notice that the ribbon matched in color the sprigs of forget-me-nots on my muslin dress. My cheeks burned, my eyes sparkled, and that singular and unaccountable feeling of "something going to happen" that seizes especially upon impressionable nature pervaded me.

Martha ran down to the pool and dipped her head into the water to cool herself. As she shook back her dripping hair and opened her eyes, there, staring at her, was what she described as the handsomest youth she had ever seen. They exchanged glances, and then, embarrassed, she ran back to her friends. The young man followed, joined the picnickers among whom he had friends, and soon was properly introduced to the girl he had so admired at the pool. His name was Benjamin

Franklin Coston, and Martha knew right then that they would marry.

Benjamin was a gifted inventor who, at 19, had been recognized by the U.S. Navy for his special talents. His proudest achievement at that time was a small submarine that could stay underwater for eight hours. Two years after they met, when Martha was 16, they eloped and secretly married because she was afraid his new navy assignment would take him away from her. Almost immediately, news of his marriage leaked out, and Benjamin arranged to have his assignment changed to a research lab at the Washington, D.C., naval yard.

During the five years that followed, Martha devoted herself to their three children, while Benjamin worked on percussion caps and cannon primers. The social life of the city was most pleasant and included friendship with Daniel Webster and Dolley Madison, who set the tone for the times and was greatly admired for the magnificence of her entertaining as well as for her charm, tact, and grace.

During their fifth year of marriage, Benjamin moved the family to Boston for business reasons. Martha was unhappy about the change, because it meant leaving the friends they had made and also because the Boston weather was so severe. Ironically, however, Boston's weather was not the problem; Washington's was. Returning from a conference in the nation's capital, Benjamin caught a cold that turned into a bad fever.

Rather than return to Boston and risk infecting his brand-new baby boy, he stopped off in Philadelphia so he could recover there.

When Coston got the news of her husband's illness, she promptly traveled to Philadelphia and took up lodgings nearby to be with him. Benjamin lingered for three months but, despite devoted care, died at the age of 26.

This was the first of an unbelievable number of tragedies that fell upon Martha in quick succession. Within weeks, her infant child died. Within the year, her mother died. And not long after, as a result of foolishness and dishonesty, Benjamin's business partners and relatives bankrupted his estate.

Virtually penniless and alone, with three children to raise and support, Martha Coston had few alternatives. She turned, for lack of any better plan, to a box of papers her husband had once mentioned as having some value. She hoped to find in it something, anything, that could help her. She approached the box carefully, little suspecting that it would change her life. But it did more than that. What she found there led to the development and manufacture of maritime signal flares still used worldwide today. They have saved thousands of lives on seagoing vessels, and some even credit the flares with helping the North win the Civil War.

In the box were many sealed and labeled packets that contained the records and plans of unfinished inventions and chemistry experiments that her husband had planned to study further. The exceptional find was an envelope containing papers describing a system of signal lights that mariners could use at night. Included was a neatly colored chart and descriptions of how to use the signals. For many years, sailing vessels had relied on a combination of colored flags and a numbered signal book. The navy had as many as 1,300 messages, each with its own individual number. When the flags were arranged in a particular fashion to represent a number, the person receiving the message had only to look in the signal book for the matching number and read what it said. It might be "Keep clear of me. I am maneuvering with difficulty" or "I am carrying mail" or any one of many important messages. The arrangement of flags could also represent a letter of the alphabet, and though spelling out a word, letter by letter, took a long time, a sailor could send a special message this way.

The problem was that no one could see the flags at night. Benjamin's idea was to use colored lights as brilliant as those he had used when he created rockets and other naval fireworks so that ships at night or in fog could signal one another at a distance. (Radio telephones were still a long way off. As a matter of fact, Alexander Bell was born the year that Martha turned 21.) Then, using maritime codes, an arrangement of lights placed high on a ship or on a land-based structure would enable an officer to convey a message of importance to another ship at sea. "I am disabled.

Communicate with me," the lights might signal, or "You are running into danger," or "You should stop your vessel immediately."

Coston knew her husband had left her a great idea. Unfortunately, he had not left one single formula for the manufacture of these theoretical signal flares. She contacted the secretary of the navy and reminded him of the navy's interest in Benjamin's signal flares. She received a letter from Admiral Hiram Paulding saying that he thought the idea was excellent and that the department encouraged her to develop it. The navy did not, however, offer to finance the development.

At that point, many people would have abandoned the project. The navy, which had regarded her husband so highly, evidenced little further interest in the signal lights, and Coston had little encouragement from other governmental sources.

As much for her husband's memory as for her own need, Martha continued to work on the signal flares, trying time and again to find some company able to formulate colors chemically with the brilliance necessary to make them visible over long distances.

And then the answer came, literally like a bolt out of the blue. Martha was in New York at the celebration of the laying of the transatlantic cable. It was an auspicious occasion, widely hailed and celebrated with a brilliant fireworks display. Watching the display, Coston realized that the men who created those brilliant colors

Hiram Paulding liked Martha Coston's proposal for colored signal flares, but neither he nor the navy did much to help her with the project.

could in all probability do the same for her signal lights. She promptly wrote for information, omitting her first name so that the men would not know that the inquiry came from a woman.

Understanding the precaution she took is easier when one realizes it was only ten years before, in 1848, that the right of women to vote in the United States was seriously considered for the first time. After the Civil

War ended, the 15th Amendment to the Constitution gave the right to vote to newly emancipated black men, but not to women. Only in 1920 did women gain the right to vote and, perhaps, to sign a business letter comfortably with their first and last name.

Martha's hunch was right. The fireworks manufacturers responded to her inquiry. She had wanted just three colors, and her first choices were red, white, and blue, like the flag. She ended up with a pure white, a brilliant red, and a vivid and unmistakable green. The manufacturers produced all three in just ten days!

When a board of naval officers tested the new lights, the report was favorable. Martha Coston was not allowed to attend the testing, of course, as only men were allowed on a naval base.

Considering the value of these new ship signals in terms of the increased safety at sea they provided and the lives they saved, the amount of money the navy paid Martha was paltry indeed: $6,000 to provide every ship in the navy with the new signals. As insurance, she secured additional patent rights for England, France, Holland, Austria, Denmark, Italy, and Sweden.

The navy's $6,000 was well spent. According to the admirals who held important commands, nearly all the captures of blockade runners during the Civil War resulted from the use of the Coston signals. However, because of wartime inflation and government price ceilings, the Coston Manufacturing Company was selling

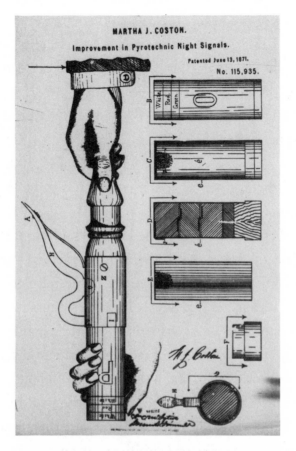

After years of hard work, Martha Coston finally received a U.S. patent for her night signals in 1871.

signals at a near loss. Determined to see the signals get the recognition and support she felt they warranted, Martha, wearing her widow's weeds, went to Europe with one of her young sons as chaperone. There she ultimately procured adoption of the signals in the French, Italian, Danish, and Swedish navies.

When she asked for $40,000 to turn over to the Union Congress all rights to her signal lights, she was paid only $20,000. Nor were they alone in treating her badly. When she asked the French government for $20,000 for patent rights, they gave her only $8,000. And when, after the war, she was entitled to $21,000 in reparations, she ended up with only $13,000. Only Denmark gave her what she considered to be fair market value.

In her memoirs, published in 1886, Coston gave her opinion of the chivalry towards women of these so-called officers and gentlemen: "Let me tell you, gentle reader, it vanishes like dew before the summer sun when one of us comes into competition with the manly sex."

Nevertheless, Coston's accomplishments were recognized worldwide. She walked with presidents and was entertained by royalty. She traveled the world in grand style and provided her family with a superb education.

Two of the Coston children grew to adulthood. William created a series of color codes that are widely used today by merchant marine and private yachts. Harry became manager of the company's manufacturing facility. He invented a pistol for firing Coston flares, which before then had been handheld. When a Lieutenant E.W. Very received a patent for improving the cartridge for the pistol, the U.S. Navy identified the entire light system that Benjamin had invented and Martha had developed and manufactured as the "Very

Pistol." Until her death, Martha Coston grieved that she was never able to have the named changed and to have credit given to her husband, her sons, and herself.

Fannie Merritt Farmer brought a scientific approach to the cooking arts.

3

Fannie Merritt Farmer

*T*reasured family recipes used to be casually handed down to anxious brides with instructions such as "add a pinch of salt" or "use enough oil to thin out the mix." Unfortunately, the results varied, sometimes disastrously, depending upon the size of the pinch and the cook's definition of how thin the mix should be.

All that changed when Fannie Merritt Farmer was asked a question by the daughter of a family friend in whose house she was working as a mother's helper. "What do you mean, add a handful of flour and a lump of butter?" asked the little girl. "How much is that?"

What *do* I mean, indeed, thought Fannie. Why not make all the ingredients in a recipe explicit and level so the finished dish turns out the same each time?

Years later, when she approached the publishers with her *Boston Cooking School Cook Book*, they were so skeptical about the exact measurements format she introduced that they insisted she pay the production costs. They little dreamed that, following its publication in 1896, the book would eventually sell four million copies! But that came later. Hard times came before.

Fannie Farmer, the inventor of the modern-day cookbook, was born on March 23, 1857, in Boston, the eldest of four girls born to John Franklin Farmer and Mary Watson Merritt Farmer. Her father, an ex-newspaperman-turned-printer, encouraged all his daughters

The cover of Fannie Merritt Farmer's best-selling book

to read. The well-to-do family spent winters in Boston and summers in Scituate. On Sunday, they attended the Unitarian Church. Afternoons were made festive with taffy pulls, and cribbage and skat were two of the games favored for evening entertainment.

Fannie's friends described her as a shy redhead. Except for some early years when they lived in Medford, Massachusetts, and she attended school there, she lived most of her life in Boston.

At 16, however, Fannie's life changed. She had just graduated from high school and was planning to go to college. And then, a "mysterious paralysis," today believed to have been polio, crippled her left leg. The paralysis left her with a permanent limp and kept her from going to college. Worse still, by the standards of the day, it made her unmarriageable. For almost ten years, Fannie was confined to bed or barely able to putter around the house. She wasn't beautiful and had no particular skills or talents. Indeed, the future looked bleak.

When the printing business run by Fannie's father began to fail in 1885, it might have been yet another discouragement for the troubled young woman. Instead, she took stock of her life, realized she would have to depend on herself to earn a living, and began to do something about her situation. She shocked the neighboring gentry when she took a job in *trade*, working behind the counter in a restaurant. But, because of

Fannie's ill health, the job proved too tiring, and she had to look elsewhere for work.

Next, Fannie found a job as a mother's helper in the home of Mrs. Charles Shaw. Fannie had never cooked much in the kitchen at home, with its huge iron stoves fed with wood and its enormous pots that one practically needed a crane to lift. But with Mrs. Shaw's support, she became quite interested in cooking. It was, she discovered, a great creative outlet. And Mrs. Shaw adored answering questions for her curious charge—questions like: "What do you mean, 'a handful'?"

With Mrs. Shaw's encouragement and the urging of her family, Fannie enrolled in the Boston Cooking School. Two years later, she finished the course, stayed on as an assistant principal, and ultimately became head of the school. Now she not only had a fine career, but she was also able to contribute generously to her family's support.

For Farmer, though, these early events were just the beginning. After eight years at the Boston Cooking School, she resigned to open her own Miss Farmer's School of Cookery. And instead of concentrating only on students who meant to be cooks or cooking teachers, she expanded her program to teach housewives and society women also. This idea was something new and quite successful. Her lectures, which included weekly demonstrations, became very popular, and homemakers (in the morning) and professional cooks (in the evening) attended them. Her recipes were regularly printed in the *Boston Transcript* and reprinted in other newspapers throughout the country.

Fannie's cookbook was published in 1896, and soon afterwards it was reprinted in England and translated into French, Spanish, and Japanese. Fannie relished its popularity, but hoped that it would be looked upon as more than a compilation of tried-and-tested recipes. She had written it in a conversational style, almost as if she were talking to a neighbor, and it reflected many of her thoughts about life.

"Cooking and eating together are among the great pleasures of family life and friendship," she wrote. She urged her readers to take pride in their kitchens and the way their tables were set. "If your table looks like a hash-house counter, you encourage people to eat accordingly," she warned.

Farmer overlooked no aspects of feeding family or guests, from thinking about what was to be prepared *before* going marketing to planning how to use leftovers! On the subject of leftovers, she had a lot to say. With imagination, she explained, they could provide the variety that engages appetites. For example, buying a pot roast twice the size needed will yield, along with some bones from the butcher, tasty makings for a fine soup. Or a fowl larger than a family can eat at a single meal can end up later in the soup pot or as chicken hash, stuffed crepes with mushrooms, and who knows what

Students carefully prepare a tray of pastries in the Fannie Farmer tradition.

else! Be thrifty, she advised, and buy what is at its peak in the market, at the best price, not what you have a sudden urge for. And cook for more than one meal at a time!

Farmer believed only in good cooking, using ingredients carefully chosen. In her view, nothing could make up for tasteless, monotonous food. She seemed able to visualize exactly how food for a particular occasion would look and taste. She had a fine sense of smell, an eye for color, and an appreciation of the different textures that could be combined to make eating interesting as well as pleasurable.

As children in childhood are taught to develop good habits, Fannie believed that adults needed to develop good cooking habits. These included learning to read recipes carefully and planning how and when to prepare meals, with an eye to what took the longest and shortest amount of time. Nothing ever needed to be wasted. Pan drippings, leftover vegetables, cooked rice—these and anything else could find their way, according to this innovator, into delicious soups, omelets, salads, and baked dishes.

Her instructions were detailed, often accompanied by friendly suggestions such as keeping a dinner party simple and resisting the temptation to scurry about and clean the last plate before sitting down with guests or family members. Throughout, she reassured her readers that making mistakes was the way that cooks learned best. Her hints were those a mother might give, and no step was too simple for her to describe in plain language.

Needless to say, Farmer took a dim view of newfangled canned foods and would probably have felt the same about the huge variety of prepared packaged foods available in stores today. One wonders what she would have thought of microwave ovens. But then, she lived at a time when very few households consisted of two adults

Fannie Farmer taught the importance of good utensils and level measurements for success in the kitchen.

working outside the home, and fast-food restaurants did not exist.

Thanks to its straightforward approach to writing recipes, Fannie Farmer's historic cookbook created a new audience. Men as well as women unabashedly turned to it for inspiration as well as instruction. It became the classic wedding gift, and no kitchen library was complete without it. More than that, it made cooking a creative activity that one could enjoy rather than a chore that had to be endured.

Counting how many cookbooks have been published since Farmer's book came out is impossible, for there are hundreds written by authors of both sexes—but her book, continually revised, is now in its 12th edition. In its original or in the current updated and revised form, it remains *the* cookbook one is likely to find in the newest and oldest of households. The publisher had updated it to reflect new equipment and new family habits, adding illustrations and even included metric equivalents. The latest edition is available in paperback and covers every aspect of cooking—from appetizers and hors d'oeuvres to cakes and candies, with stops at everthing from marinades to relishes and pasta.

And lest there be any question unanswered about any meal of the the day or week, her cookbook also provides informative guides to menu planning for family and friends, including dinner parties, cocktail parties and receptions, buffet dinners, picnics and barbecues, and communal dinners—all with a gentle reminder of the secret of entertaining: If you try to please your guests as you would your family, you'll realize that it is not necessary to do something extravagant to impress. Simplicity, using good ingredients well, is usually more impressive than a lot of fancy cooking that is sometimes too much to handle when you are doing everything yourself. Serve dishes that you know you can manage, and plan ahead so that you can enjoy your own guests.

However popular her cookbook was, Fannie felt it had a further purpose and that was, in her words, "to awaken deeper thought and broader study of what to eat." She anticipated today's tremendous surge of interest in the benefits of a sound diet and its relation to good health. More and more, she became interested in the subject of diet for people who were ill. She began to give short courses to hospital nurses on invalid and dietetic cookery. She wrote another cookbook, published in 1904, entitled *Food and Cookery for the Sick and Convalescent* and even trained hospital dieticians and lectured at the Harvard Medical School.

Fannie's extensive involvement with diet for the sick brought her into contact with Dr. Elliott P. Joslin, then pioneering the study of diabetes, who credited her with stimulating him to write about the disease.

Despite her condition from her childhood polio, Fannie was tireless. In her later years she lectured to women's clubs and groups throughout the country. Although she was somewhat plump and plain looking, even severe, because of the pince-nez glasses she always wore, and rather reserved in social situations, she sparkled on the lecture platform. It was her medium. Even when two strokes confined her to a wheelchair, she continued to lecture to audiences eager to listen to her.

For ten years, with the assistance of her sister Cora, Fannie wrote a monthly page in the *Woman's Home Companion*, one of the most popular publications of the day. But that wasn't all. Between the years 1898 and 1912, along with her other activities, she managed to

48

write several other successful cookbooks, including *Chafing Dish Possibilities*, *What to Have for Dinner*, and *A New Book of Cookery*.

Fannie Farmer died in Boston on January 15, 1915, at the age of 58, a household name known to millions of grateful brides, bachelors, and anyone else who has ever had to prepare a dish from a printed recipe. Her name has lived on, though with a slightly different spelling, in the Fanny Farmer Candy Shops, a chain of stores specializing in chocolates that was founded four years after her death and now has more than 300 locations throughout the United States.

Only one generation removed from slavery, Madam C.J. Walker overcame poverty to become one of the wealthiest women in the United States.

4

Madam C.J. Walker

*I*n 1887, when she was barely 20 years old, Sarah Breedlove was faced with a decision that she knew would change her life. The first free child of African-American slaves, Sarah had already been forced to make many tough choices in her life. Orphaned at age 7, married at 14, and a mother at 17, she was far more adult than her age implied. But this decision was different. Recently widowed, Sarah, a washerwoman, was now solely responsible for the welfare of her baby daughter, A'Lelia. And she desperately wanted to create a life for A'Lelia that was better than her own.

The decision was whether to stay in the Mississippi town of Vicksburg, where she had lived in and around most of her life, or to move to the big city of St. Louis, Missouri. Sarah had heard that washerwomen could find work there, and a friend of hers had relatives in St. Louis who might take them in as borders. With just enough money to buy a one-way boat ticket, she knew the wrong decision could be disastrous.

Sarah made her decision. She and A'Lelia would leave home and go to St. Louis to start a new life. Twenty years later, Sarah, or Madam C. J. Walker as she would then be called, became the first African-American woman to become a millionaire, owning a cosmetics company that employed hundreds of people. She became a role model not only for men and women of her own race, but also for all would-be entrepreneurs. What's more, she helped nurture the early development of the civil rights movement by contributing her energy and money to many African-American political and social causes.

The rags-to-riches story of Madam C. J. Walker is one of the greatest examples of the "American Dream." Looking back to earlier days, she recalled how discouraged she would become. "As I bent over the washboard and looked at my arms buried in the soapsuds, I said to myself, 'What are you going to do when you grow old and your back gets stiff?' This set me to thinking, but with all my thinking, I couldn't see how I, a poor washerwoman, was going to better my condition." Discouraged but never defeated, Sarah's can-do spirit carried her through the hard times.

Madam C. J. Walker was born Sarah Breedlove on a

plantation in Louisiana, in 1867, two years after the end of the Civil War had freed her parents from slavery. Despite their newly won freedom, life had changed very little for Owen and Minerva Breedlove. True, they lived in one of the most prosperous farming communities in the country, where the rich soil produced bountiful crops of cotton. But like most former slaves, the Breedloves were sharecroppers, or tenant farmers. Because they didn't own the land they farmed, almost all the crops they raised went directly to the wealthy white landlords, most of whom were former slave owners. Life was so hard that Minerva worked in the fields picking cotton until the day before she give birth to Sarah.

As soon as Sarah was old enough, probably when she was four or five, she joined her parents and her older brother and sister, Alex and Louvenia, in the fields. On a typical day, Sarah would rise at dawn to help her mother and sister make breakfast and begin preparing that night's supper. In the evenings, after helping in the fields all day, she would do her household chores: feeding the chickens, sweeping, helping to serve supper, and so on. Saturdays were reserved for laundry. She would help her mother earn a few extra pennies by washing clothes for white customers in big wooden tubs with washboards. Though her illiterate parents longed for their children to be educated, there simply was no time for school.

In 1874, when Sarah was seven years old, a yellow

fever epidemic swept across the Mississippi River delta. Hundreds died, including Sarah's parents. With Owen and Minerva gone, the burden of supporting the family fell to Alex. The Breedlove children tried to work the farmland themselves, but failed. This forced Alex to move to Vicksburg to find work, leaving Louvenia and Sarah alone on the farm, where they earned barely enough to feed themselves by doing laundry.

Four years later, yellow fever struck again. To make matters worse, the cotton crop failed. People could no longer afford to pay Sarah and Louvenia to wash their clothes. Without a source of income, the girls lost their home. In the hope of finding work, they moved to Vicksburg to join their brother. When Louvenia married soon after, Sarah moved in with the couple in a old shack, but her brother-in-law was anything but kind to her.

Longing for her own home, Sarah married a Vicksburg laborer, Moses McWilliams, when she was only 14. She helped her husband support themselves by taking in laundry, as she had since she was a little girl. When she was 17, Sarah gave birth to her daughter. Two years later, Moses died in an accident.

Upon arriving in St. Louis with A'Lelia in 1888, Sarah found a lifestyle far different from the small town atmosphere of Vicksburg. St. Louis, nicknamed "The Gateway City," was a noisy, bustling metropolis of a half-million people on the edge of the developing

American frontier. Every day, immigrants from around the world, as well as southern blacks, poured into the city by the hundreds. There were newfangled inventions like electric lights and streetcars and enormous factories that produced everything from beer to plows. And people were dancing and listening to a crazy new music called ragtime. St. Louis thrived on new ideas.

While Sarah continued to work long hours as a washerwoman, she had to admit life was better than what she had known back home. For one thing, she earned enough so that A'Lelia didn't have to work during the school year. In fact, she had even scrimped enough so that when A'Lelia graduated from high school, she could afford to send her to Knoxville College, a small African-American institution in Tennessee. This was no small achievement for a black washerwoman and single mother whose parents had been slaves.

In 1904, St. Louis hosted the World's Fair. As part of the festivities, many black intellectuals appeared and gave speeches. This was Sarah's first exposure to such great African-Americans as poet Paul Laurence Dunbar, author and political activist W. E. B. DuBois, and educator Booker T. Washington. But it was the appearance of Mrs. Booker T. Washington—Margaret Murray Washington—that impressed Sarah the most. Mrs. Washington was articulate, worldly, and extremely well groomed—everything she herself was not, thought the

Madam C.J. Walker's daughter, A'Lelia, as an adult

37-year-old Sarah. Now that she had laid a foundation
for her daughter's success, she vowed to improve herself.

Whether because of poor diet or too much work,
Sarah's hair had begun to fall out—a major obstacle on
her road to self-improvement. She tried various hair
tonics but none of them worked, and she grew discouraged. One evening in 1905, she would recall, God

Booker T. Washington and his wife, Margaret, strongly inspired the woman who was to become Madam C.J. Walker.

answered her prayer. "I had a dream, and in that dream a big black man appeared to me and told me what to mix up for my hair. Some of the remedy was grown in Africa, but I sent for it, mixed it, put it on my scalp, and in a few weeks my hair was coming in faster than it had ever fallen out. . . . I tried it on my friends; it helped them. I made up my mind I would begin to sell it."

Unfortunately, the Poro Company, manufacturer of a product called the "Wonder Hair Grower," was based in St. Louis. Deciding that her competing product stood a better chance in a different city, Sarah packed her bags and moved to Denver. In a sense, Denver had become what St. Louis had been 18 years earlier when Sarah had moved there—the gateway to the American frontier. It was the perfect place to begin a new venture and a new life, thought Sarah. With A'Lelia still in college, her only regret in leaving St. Louis was leaving Charles Joseph Walker, a sales agent for a local newspaper with whom she had become close friends.

Arriving in Denver with only $1.50 in savings, Sarah had to get work immediately. She found a job as a cook with a prominent businessman named E. L. Scholtz, who owned Colorado's largest and most modern pharmacy. (Chances are that she probably consulted with Mr. Scholtz and his staff when first developing her hair lotions.) Finally, she saved enough money to pay for her rent and devoted herself to perfecting three products: Wonderful Hair Grower, Glossine, and Vegetable Shampoo.

Sarah's secret-formula hair products, designed expressly for black women, proved to be an immediate success in Denver. The lotions not only thoroughly and gently cleansed hair, but also softened the naturally tight curls of her customers, allowing them to wear the long, flowing hairdos popular at the turn of the century.

Wonderful Hair Grower—one of Walker's earliest and most successful products

She expanded her market rapidly by taking out ads in the *Colorado Statesman*, the African-American newspaper published in Denver. Soon her products were the talk of Colorado.

Sarah continued her friendship with Charles Walker by mail, relying on his salesmanship to guide her own burgeoning business. One day Charles arrived in Denver, and the two close friends decided to marry. Their wedding took place on January 4, 1906. As Mr. Walker's new wife, Sarah had her name officially changed to Mrs. C. J. Walker. To suggest a touch of elegance to her products, she added "Madam" to their labels.

By 1906, Sarah was ready to expand Madam C. J. Walker's hair products beyond Denver. Although her husband advised against it, warning that such a venture would spell financial ruin for their new company, Madam Walker embarked on an ambitious cross-country tour to establish sales offices. She spent a year and a half on the road, hiring and training sales agents—black women like herself—as far away as New York. Sales began to flood in.

By 1908, her vast mail-order business prompted Madam Walker to move her company headquarters to a location that was more central to the population centers of the United States at that time. She chose Pittsburgh, a thriving banking and industrial city. A'Lelia joined her mother to help run the business, and together they opened a training school for Walker sales agents, which they called Lelia College.

A school for sales agents was a revolutionary concept for business, one that would be copied many times over. At Lelia College, students learned about the products and about the door-to-door sales techniques, which Madam Walker was the first to introduce on an organized, large-scale basis. Upon graduation, the Walker sales agents were immediately recognizable, with their carefully coiffed hair and their uniforms of black skirts and starched white blouses.

Walker sales agents learned about the company's many products through classroom demonstrations.

Once again, business grew so quickly that the Walker company soon outgrew its facilities. Looking for a permanent location to build the company's first factory, Madam Walker decided upon Indianapolis, which had become the country's largest inland manufacturing center. In 1911, one year after setting up headquarters in Indianapolis, the Walker company proudly announced that its national sales forces consisted of 950 agents and a monthly income of $1,000, which was a substantial amount of money when the average income for white unskilled workers was only $45 monthly.

While Madam Walker had become one of the city's most prominent business owners, she, like other African-Americans, faced discrimination. One day, simply because she was black, she was charged more than twice the standard admission of white patrons to a local movie theater. She promptly hired an attorney and sued the theater. What's more, she immediately began plans for creating a block-long entertainment and business complex called "The Walker Building" in downtown Indianapolis. The complex, which included an elegant movie theater, was built some years later.

The next seven years saw the Walker company continue to grow. Following her divorce from Charles, largely over differences in running the business, Madam herself conducted sales trips to the Caribbean and Central America to expand her business internationally. Following a visit to New York City, A'Lelia convinced

The Walker Building and Walker Theatre in Indianapolis

her mother to move the company headquarters to
Harlem, the vibrant center of African-American culture.
The fashionable Walker beauty salon became the toast
of Harlem, and Madam Walker constructed a fabulous
mansion on the Hudson River, which rivaled any in
New York. By 1918, with sales of the Walker company
exceeding $250,000 annually, Madam Walker officially
had become the country's first black woman millionaire.

The re-election of Woodrow Wilson in 1916
prompted Walker to become a political activist. She
had always been a generous contributor and tireless
worker for numerous charitable organizations for the
needy. While considered progressive in many other

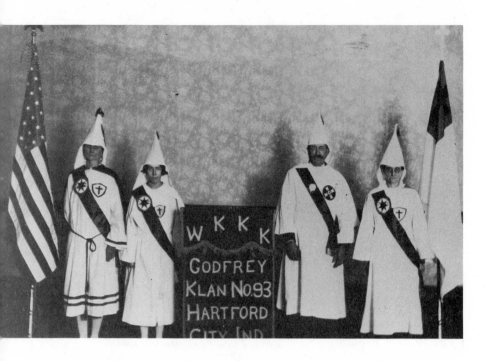

Madam C.J. Walker strenuously fought against racial hatred, including the violent activities of the Ku Klux Klan.

ways, Wilson, the first southern president since the Civil War, was a segregationist and rolled back many of the reforms that had given American blacks new hope for equal rights. Wilson was also reluctant to offend his fellow southern politicians by speaking out against the heinous lynchings and other notorious murders conducted by the white supremacist group, the Ku Klux Klan, which claimed the lives of 3,000 blacks between 1885 and 1916. Walker became increasingly outspoken against racial inequality and was among the prominent blacks who paid a highly publicized visit to the White House in 1917 to protest the lynchings.

Madam Walker died on May 25, 1919. In her will, she named her daughter A'Lelia as her principal heir, but among the beneficiaries were scores of charitable and educational organizations, including the National Association of American Colored People and Tuskegee Institute, the African-American university founded by Booker T. Washington. Many mourned her death, but perhaps the most eloquent of them was W. E. B. Du-Bois, who in his obituary for her wrote, "It is given to few persons to transform a people in a generation. Yet this was done by the late Madam C. J. Walker."

Dr. Sara Josephine Baker's medical practices improved the health of millions of New Yorkers.

5

S. Josephine Baker

*O*ne of Sara Josephine Baker's earliest childhood memories was about the impulse to help. Little Josephine was all dressed up for a great occasion in her finest outfit: a white lace dress with a blue sash, light blue silk stockings, and light blue kid-leather shoes. She looked like a model for the upper-class Victorian American child that she was. While waiting for her mother to get ready, Josephine wandered across her big front yard and sat by the road, hoping someone would stop to admire her. She didn't have to wait long, for soon a poor black girl, about the same age, arrived. Josephine remembered her as dressed in rags and looking hungry. With hardly a moment's thought, Josephine took off all her clothes—including her new kid-leather shoes—and gave them to the other little girl, who was very grateful. Josephine returned to her home naked, but her loving parents understood why she had helped the other child.

That same desire to help the poor—especially children—would inspire Sara Josephine Baker throughout her life. In 1898, a time when women were not even allowed to vote, she would become one of the first women medical doctors in the United States. Despite her privileged background, she enthusiastically worked to take care of children in the world's worst ghettos. When she saw the need for a new type of baby garment that would help prevent accidental suffocation and a new type of eye drops for babies that would help prevent blindness, she became an inventor.

Later, she would organize the first governmental agency devoted exclusively to children's health. This agency served as a model for other international organizations. By the time she officially retired in 1923, her pioneering work in child hygiene had saved over 80,000 lives.

Born on November 15, 1873, in Poughkeepsie, New York, Sara Josephine Baker was the third daughter and the fourth child of Orlando D. Baker, a well-to-do lawyer, and his wife, Jenny. Her father came from Quaker stock, and her mother was a descendant of one of the founders of Harvard University. Both strongly believed in instilling in all of their children the value of a well-rounded education in the arts and sciences. In fact, Mrs. Baker held the unusual distinction for women of her day of holding a college degree, having entered the very first class of Vassar College.

As a child, Josephine's life in Poughkeepsie was idyllic—filled with candy pulls, formal luncheons, afternoon teas and dances. During the summer, children picnicked and fished in the nearby Catskill Mountains. In the fall and winter, they went on hayrides or did winter skating and ice yachting. And as a special treat, the whole family would take a boat ride to New York City, just down the Hudson River, to attend the latest plays on Broadway. Josephine learned how to can jams and bake, although she never really had to cook because the family's large, two-story home was run by servants.

When Josephine was 16, her life abruptly changed. In the course of less than three months, her beloved brother Robert, 13, and then her father died in a typhoid fever epidemic. (Typhoid is a disease frequently carried through drinking water. At the time, the town of Poughkeepsie drew its water directly from the Hudson, which was becoming increasingly polluted by the farms and factories upstream.) The discovery that the family had very little in savings compounded the tragedy.

Josephine abandoned her plans to follow in her mother's footsteps at Vassar and decided that instead she needed to find a way to support herself and her family. But her choice of becoming a physician astounded everyone. "There was no medical tradition on either side of my family. There were lawyers but no doctors. And both sides of the family were aghast at the idea of my spending so much money in such . . . a harebrained and unwomanly scheme," she recalled later in her autobiography, *Fighting for Life*. Today, the prospect of a young woman entering medical school seems perfectly normal. But in the late 1800s, it was almost unheard of. Even her family doctor scolded her for considering such an outrageous idea. Nevertheless, Josephine had made up her mind and eventually her native New England stubbornness won over her mother, who consented to finance her daughter's medical school with $5,000 from the family's rapidly diminishing fortune.

In 1898, Josephine entered the Woman's Medical College of New York, one of the few medical schools that enrolled women. One course in particular—about children's mental and physical health—would have a lasting impact on her life. The class was innovative because, at that time, the medical profession made no distinction between children's and adult's health care. Ironically, she was initially bored by the subject matter and failed the course the first time around. "That was my first, and only failure (in medical school). It . . . gave a severe jolt to my pride." She resolutely took the course over again and, when she gave it a chance, found it fascinating.

Josephine's first introduction to the abject poverty of

turn-of-the-century urban slums was during her medical internship for a Boston hospital. There, the proper young physician-in-training encountered what she would remember as "the dregs of Boston, ignorant, shiftless, settled irrevocably into surly degradation. Just to make sure they would be hopeless, many of them drank savagely."

With her internship completed, Josephine could now officially hang up her shingle as Dr. Baker. She moved to New York City in 1900 to set up a private practice—and then waited for the patients to pour into her office. Unfortunately, the idea of a woman doctor was no more popular in the big city than it had been back home. During her first year in business, she made only $185, although on one occasion she did attend to the needs of the most famous woman of her day, the great actress and singer Lillian Russell.

To make extra money, Dr. Baker applied for a job as a city medical inspector. Because she applied as "Dr. S. J. Baker," city officials assumed she was a man and hired her. When they later discovered, much to their chagrin, that they had just hired their first woman for that position, Dr. Baker had already become a civil servant, which protected her from being fired.

The city assigned Baker to the task of inspecting health conditions in the worst slum in the city. Nicknamed "Hell's Kitchen," the ghetto was filled with recently arrived immigrants from Europe, escaping

Early in Dr. Baker's medical career, she took care of the flamboyant actress, Lillian Russell (1861-1922).

famine and political upheavals, as well as poor black southerners. The ghetto had one of the highest infant mortality rates in the world. During summer months, when disease was especially prevalent, as many as 1,500 babies died every week in an area of less than one square mile. Day after day, Baker would climb the steps of decrepit tenements teeming with vermin and filled with nauseating smells to witness and account for the dying children. "I had a sincere conviction that [the slum dwellers] would be better off dead than so degradingly alive," she would recall later. Among the residents was the infamous "Typhoid Mary," a knowing disease carrier who willfully infected several dozen people. Dr. Baker helped to apprehend her.

Despite their poverty, the inhabitants of Hell's Kitchen had a zest for life that impressed Baker, and she

In making her inspection rounds, Dr. Baker often came upon piles of garbage left out in the open.

Masses of people living and working in crowded quarters contributed greatly to the widespread health problems that Dr. Baker battled in New York. This photograph shows part of the city's East Side in 1912.

was very much determined to help them. Many of the diseases that afflicted them—such as typhoid, influenza, dysentery, and tuberculosis—had no cures yet, and treatment was limited. But Baker called upon the wise advice of the eighteenth-century Boston printer, Benjamin Franklin, who had said many years before that an ounce of prevention was worth a pound of cure. In the summer of 1908, she and a team of 30 trained nurses began an experiment aimed at testing the effectiveness of *preventative* medicine, an entirely new idea at the time. They taught the ghetto dwellers such basic principles as proper ventilation, bathing, and suitable clothing. They encouraged mothers to breast-feed their babies to avoid the dangers of bottled milk, which at that time was still unpasteurized. And they taught young mothers how to sanitize cooking utensils by boiling them in water.

By the end of the summer, the results of their efforts were dramatic—1,200 fewer babies died than in the previous summer. City officials were so impressed that they opened the world's first public health agency devoted exclusively to improving children's health and appointed Dr. Baker as its chief executive. Her appointment made her the only woman in the United States to head up an entire department for a big city.

However, despite her authority, Dr. Baker still faced severe prejudice because she was a woman. In fact, six male doctors on her staff threatened to resign rather than work for a woman. In response, Dr. Baker struck a bargain with them: if after working for her for 30 days they still wanted to resign, she would personally help them find other positions. At the end of the month, the men decided that they didn't mind working for Dr. Baker after all, and all remained on her staff.

That incident left its mark on Dr. Baker. Later the

same year, she and a group of other college-educated women founded the College Equal Suffrage League, an early women's rights group. Their first goal was getting women the right to vote.

Dr. Baker's Bureau of Child Hygiene started a number of programs that would be copied around the world. Baby health stations, which dispensed fresh milk and free infant care information to mothers, were set up throughout the ghettos. These were followed by dental clinics, where schoolchildren were introduced to the toothbrush. When Baker realized that the eldest daughters of many poor families were forced to take charge of their younger siblings while both parents worked, she established "Little Mothers' League." This group gave the girls practical advice on feeding, exercising, dressing, and other aspects of baby care.

To marshal public support for her programs, Baker established the Children's Welfare Federation, which coordinated the work of private organizations interested in helping ghetto children. And to disseminate information about child hygiene to other parts of the country, she co-founded the American Child Hygiene Association in 1909 and vowed that she would not retire until a children's health agency was established in every state. Over the next five years, Dr. Baker, by all accounts a witty and natural speaker, gave lectures on children's health throughout the United States.

About this time, Baker became aware of the fact that

The building that housed Dr. Baker's Bureau of Child Hygiene in New York City

babies were accidentally being suffocated by the elaborate infant clothing that was the fashion of the day. Although she was hardly a seamstress, her Yankee ingenuity guided her in creating simple baby wear that opened from the front—a first. The Metropolitan Life Insurance Company was so impressed that it bought and distributed 200,000 of the sewing patterns.

When Dr. Baker learned that the silver nitrate eye drops given to all newborn babies to help prevent blindness from gonorrheal infection was actually causing some babies to be blinded, she again became an inventor. Stored in bottles, the solution would evaporate allowing the active ingredient to rise to dangerously high levels. Her answer was simple: put the solution in beeswax capsules. This would prevent evaporation, automatically regulate the proper amount dispensed, and keep the solution sterile. Dr. Baker's capsules are still used around the world.

In 1916, in the middle of World War I, Dr. Baker noticed that many of the donations that had helped poor children were now being redirected overseas to the war effort. Her controversial statement that "it's six times safer to be a soldier in the trenches of France than to be born a baby in the United States" got the American public's attention about the continuing needs of its poor children. To improve their nutrition, she established a wartime children's program that is a model for today's school lunch program.

Dr. Josephine Baker a few years before her death

That same year, Baker received an invitation from the dean of the New York University-Bellevue Hospital Medical School to lecture on child hygiene as part of a new doctorate degree being created in public health. Receiving such an offer from one of the leaders of the medical establishment was quite an honor, although Dr. Baker was eminently qualified. Dr. Baker accepted, but on one condition: she be allowed to enroll as a student.

Not only would she be able to earn her own doctorate in public health, but more importantly, she would also break the school's ban on female students. At first, the dean refused, but eventually, when he realized that no one else could teach the course as knowledgeably as Dr. Baker, he gave in to her request. One year later, Baker became the first woman to graduate from the school and the first to receive a doctorate in public health. After the prestigious New York University medical school began admitting female students, other medical schools around the country followed suit.

Over the next few years, Dr. Baker divided her time between running the Bureau of Child Hygiene, consulting with public health officials around the world, and promoting women's rights. In 1918, she was among the women invited to the White House by President Woodrow Wilson to discuss women's suffrage. At the end of the meeting, President Wilson solidly endorsed the concept, and in 1920 the 19th Amendment became law, officially allowing women the right to vote.

In 1923, Dr. Baker officially retired, having achieved her goal that every state establish a child hygiene department. She went to work as a consultant with the League of Nations, the forerunner of the United Nations, and wrote several books on children's health. She also wrote her autobiography—which many readers of the day at first thought was the story of Josephine Baker, the famed jazz dancer. (Because the two names were so similar, Dr. Baker always referred to herself as S. Josephine Baker.) Dr. Baker died on February 22, 1945, but her pioneering work in child hygiene lives on today, in everything from school lunch programs to the United Nations Children's Fund (UNICEF).

Barbara McClintock, at work in 1947 behind her microscope, shows the intense concentration that characterized her life as a scientist.

6

Barbara McClintock

*A*s a child, Barbara McClintock was somewhat of a loner. She liked nothing better than curling up with a good book or spending an afternoon alone, traipsing about some undiscovered territory. In fact, she so enjoyed being left to her own devices that her mother worried about her. In 1908, when she was not yet six years old, she was sent to live with her aunt and uncle while her mother coped with her three younger siblings at home. All she had to say when she returned six months later was, "I enjoyed myself very much and was absolutely not homesick!"

Barbara wasn't anti-social; she simply found pleasure in her own company and enjoyed exploring the world around her. Her stoic personality would serve her well when she later became a scientist specializing in genetics. For decades, she studied the development of cell structure by tending a field of corn. Her findings would revolutionize biology and change forever our concepts of the way living things pass along their physical traits to their offspring. Upon granting her the coveted Nobel Prize in Medicine and Physiology, the awards

Much of Barbara McClintock's research took place in the cornfields she tended.

committee declared that her work "in genetics was one of the two great discoveries of our time."

Born on June 16, 1902, in Hartford, Connecticut, Barbara and her family moved to Brooklyn when she was young. There she and her siblings attended elementary school and later went to Erasmus Hall High School. Summers, in what was still wild and unspoiled Long Beach a few hours away, gave Barbara what she longed for—more opportunities to be by herself.

Despite her mother's misgivings, her father encouraged Barbara's inquisitive mind. And both parents held rather unorthodox viewpoints on the value of public education, regarding school as just a small part of growing up. Barbara loved learning, but was often absent from school. Instead she skated, played ball, and climbed trees! Dr. McClintock even made clear to the school officials that "his children were not to be given homework—six hours a day of school were more than enough!"

As Barbara got older, her mother felt that her daughter had to stop being a tomboy. Neither did she care for the fact that this oldest daughter enjoyed science and solving problems, and thought about going to college. In her view, girls shouldn't like such things. But life changed when World War I began and the army sent Dr. McClintock overseas as a military surgeon. Money became very short, and Barbara's mother had to teach piano to earn what the family needed.

Now 16 and a high school graduate, with Cornell University very much on her mind, Barbara despaired of going to college, not only because her mother disapproved, but also because they simply couldn't afford the expense. Instead, determined to get an education, she worked at an employment agency and spent evenings in the library reading and studying.

Six months later, her father returned from the war and convinced her mother that going to college was important for Barbara. Barbara always suspected her last-minute application to Cornell and prompt acceptance had been smoothed by her mother, who felt that if her brilliant daughter was going to apply, she'd see the right people and make certain there would be no problem about her admission.

Cornell proved to be all Barbara had hoped for. Although she had enrolled in the College of Agriculture because the tuition was free, she took many kinds of courses, continuing if she was stimulated by them or dropping those that proved to be uninteresting. The registrar's office complained and put off the date of her graduation, but Barbara didn't worry about the future.

At Cornell, Barbara blossomed socially. She dated, was elected president of the women's freshman class, and rushed by a sorority—an invitation she declined when her Jewish roommates were passed over. She even had her long hair shingled, a daring move for the times although the hair style soon became fashionable.

But something much more significant happened to Barbara: she developed a passion for a subject that would absorb her completely for the rest of her life. It was cytology—the branch of biology that deals with the structure, function, and life history of cells and the nature of their diseases, causes, and symptoms. Her professors were supportive and appreciative of her talents, so much so that by the time she was a graduate student, she moved from being an assistant to working on her own.

In 1927, Barbara completed her graduate work at Cornell, received her Ph.D. in botany, and was made an instructor. But she was eager for more. "What I wanted to do was something that is so obvious now it seems incredible that it was not obvious to the geneticists or plant breeders at Cornell at the time," she said.

Her study involved genes—the elements by which hereditary characteristics are determined and transmitted—and chromosomes, which carry those genes. The generally accepted theory of the day was that genes were permanently attached to chromosomes in a strict, straight line "like pearls on a string" and that the inherited characteristics that resulted were predictable and logical. However, Dr. McClintock's pioneering research with corn kernels and maize plants convinced her that genes could "jump" and make changes in the "string of pearls" and that those changes accounted for differences in the color of the corn kernels her plants produced in

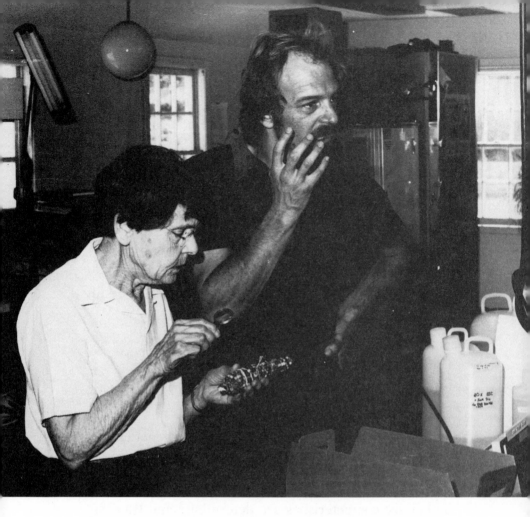

With colleagues in her laboratory, Dr. McClintock examines kernels of corn.

successive generations. She gave the name *transposition* to the "jump" that took place.

This theory offered an astounding explanation of the previously unexplained fact that genes in plants, animals, and humans "jumped" and changed predicted and logical characteristics. But her explanation was vigorously rejected by many people, even laughed at by some. "They thought I was quite mad," said Dr. McClintock.

In 1983, when she was awarded her Nobel Prize, the awards committee was not surprised that her theories had been rejected for decades. In their view, only about five geneticists in the world could understand and appreciate Dr. McClintock's theories because of the complexities of the work. And yet, her work had some

In an auditorium in Stockholm, Sweden, Barbara McClintock receives her 1983 Nobel Prize in physiology.

very practical applications, including the study of antibi-
otic-resistant bacteria, the finding of a cure for African
sleeping sickness, and inroads in the study of cancer.

Despite her revolutionary research, however, the
academic world was not ready for a woman with uncon-
ventional thoughts. Had Dr. McClintock been a man,
she would in all probability have received a proper faculty appointment. But not until 1947 did Cornell
appoint its first woman assistant professor in a field
other than home economics. Because she wanted most
of all to have the time for and a place to work, Dr.
McClintock had accepted being passed over. But now
she felt the time had come to leave the university.

For the next two years, with the aid of a fellowship
from the National Research Council, she traveled to
other universities. But Cornell continued to serve as
her home base, where she could check on her crops.
"They couldn't supply me with a job, but they supplied
me with everything else," she explained.

At Cornell, women were not permitted to hold
tenured professorships, no matter how many degrees
they had. Dr. McClintock found herself without a job a
number of times during the ten-year period after she
received her Ph.D. Part of that was due to her reputation as a loner and a maverick, something that stemmed
from her insistence that she could relate to more conventional scientists without the obligation of sharing all
their assumptions. Nevertheless, her male colleagues

found jobs, and *that* she felt was wholly unfair. What never seriously crossed her mind, however, was the thought of a specific commitment to a career. She thought only of her research. "I was so interested in what I was doing, I could hardly wait to get up in the morning and get at it."

In 1942, Dr. McClintock was outright unemployed. However, one of her many supporters from among the people with whom she worked was Lewis Stadler, a fellow geneticist who was on the faculty of the University of Missouri. When he was awarded an $80,000 grant from the Rockefeller Foundation to build a major center of genetics at the university, he secured for Dr. McClintock the position of assistant professor—her first offer of a faculty position. The job both pleased and displeased her. She was happy to have a place to continue her research, but she resented the fact that her appointment was made possible only through influence, not solely on the basis of her ability. No chance existed, she thought, of being promoted.

And so, after five years, she again left a university she had hoped to call home, depressed and with her morale at its lowest point. What she needed now was a place to work and a field in which to grow corn to continue her research. The problem was, where?

The answer came from a geneticist friend who said he planned to go out to Cold Spring Harbor on Long Island to grow his corn. He'd be happy, he said, to see that she got an invitation to stay the summer. Dr. McClintock hardly suspected that, despite her reluctance to commit herself to anything, she would ultimately become a permanent resident of an institute that each summer attracted 60 or more geneticists and fellow scientists of both orthodox and new schools of thought. There, working alone for more than 40 years, she rediscovered and fully developed the theories about transposition regarding the changes in the "string of pearls" that she had arrived at earlier. Most important, her studies revealed to her how complex genetic organization is and how naive humans are to underestimate the flexibility of living organisms.

"Plants," said McClintock, "are extraordinary. For instance . . . if you pinch a leaf of a plant you set off electric pulses. . . . There is no question that plants have all kinds of sensitivities. They do a lot of responding to their environment. . . ."

In 1951, during the Cold Spring Harbor Symposium, Dr. McClintock made the first formal presentation of her theory of transposition. The response, with few exceptions, was hostile. The complaint was that the theory was impossible to understand. Five years later, a second presentation, based on mechanisms of plant control and regulation that she had unraveled, received even less approval. Only two members of the audience wrote to ask for reprints of her article.

In the many years that followed, during which she

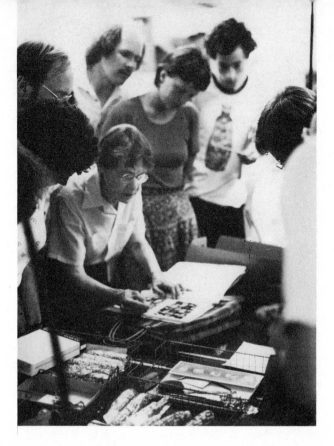

Many students in Professor McClintock's seminars and plant classes benefited from her years of field research.

continued to do almost all her research alone, her style remained her own, less and less influenced by others. Her views of what was important continued to differ from those of others in the field. The result made her more and more of a loner. Whereas prior to her second Cold Spring Harbor presentation she had enjoyed visits from colleagues from all over the world, attended meetings, and responded to invitations to give seminars, now she retreated into her laboratory at Cold Spring Harbor to work without interruption.

Barbara McClintock led a life rich in both personal satisfaction and contributions to the world of science.

Her work required an extraordinary amount of patience. In her biography, *A Feeling for the Organism: The Life and Work of Barbara McClintock*, Evelyn Fox Keller described how Dr. McClintock spent her days:

Corn genetics is hard work. To prolong the growing season, it is necessary to plant the corn in the warmest spot available—usually a hollow facing south. As the summer progresses, the heat can become oppressive. Work begins early in the morning, before it gets too hot, but continues throughout the day. The young plants need constant watering; they must not be allowed to dry out. Each one is tagged and watched carefully, both in the fields and in the laboratory. When the time for fertilization arrives, utmost precaution must be taken to prevent a chance pollination.

Recognition and honors, however, mounted with the years. By 1981, when she was 79, these honors included the prestigious $15,000 Lasker Award For Basic Medical Research; a $50,000 prize from Israel's Wolf Foundation; and the First Prize Fellow Laureate of Chicago's MacArthur Foundation, which provided her with a lifelong annual tax-free income of $60,000.

Barbara McClintock died on September 2, 1992, but who could not help being envious of this remarkable scientist, a woman who summed up her life's work by saying, "Working in my corn patch has been such a deep pleasure that I never thought of stopping and I just hated sleeping. I can't imagine having a better life."

While working as a single mother, Bette Nesmith Graham invented a product that would make her and her son millionaires.

7

Bette Nesmith Graham

*B*ette Nesmith's mother called her "independent and strong-willed." But her teachers called her stubborn and a troublemaker, and school discipline didn't sit well with Bette. She dropped out at 17 and applied for a secretarial job at a law firm, even though she didn't know how to type. Luckily, the firm liked her quick, bright mind and took her on part time. The firm never suspected that, a few years later, Bette would invent a product that would forever revolutionize the typing pool and make her a heroine to secretaries everywhere.

The creator of Liquid Paper correction fluid was a working single mother in the 1950s when—through persistence and resourcefulness—she parlayed a good idea into a $40 million corporation. Her legacy remains in the several foundations she created to support women's artistic and social causes and in the work of her son, Michael Nesmith, the former guitarist of the 1960s chart toppers, "The Monkees." An inheritance helped finance his innovative work in music video and career as a filmmaker.

Bette came from an ordinary background. She wasn't a genius and never went to college. Born Bette Claire McMurray on March 23, 1924, in Dallas, Texas, she and her sister, Yvonne, who was two years younger, lived in a middle-class neighborhood with their parents, Jesse and Christine McMurray.

Jesse was in the wholesale auto business, but it was Christine, a self-taught painter, singer and business-woman—as well as a wife and mother—who by her example instilled in Bette the notion that motherhood did not necessarily mean sacrificing career. Christine had her own local radio program and even sang on it from time to time. She also opened a knitting shop to teach needlework and sell her wares with the help of the nurse who had taught her to knit. Such behavior was advanced for its time, but that ran in the family. Bette's great-great grandfather, John Darby, was co-founder of Wesleyan College in Macon, Georgia, one of the first women's colleges in the country.

At 18, Bette married Warren Nesmith, a National Guardsman. However, after only two months of marriage, Warren was called to duty when Pearl Harbor was bombed. The honeymoon period was just long enough for her to conceive her son, Michael. At 19, she was facing life alone as a war bride with a baby on the way.

War is hard on separated couples, and when, after three years in the service, Warren returned, things did not go well. Bette and Warren divorced a year later.

Raising her son as a single mother and working at the same time, Bette had good reason to be proud when she left the typing pool to become an executive secretary for the chairman of the Texas Bank & Trust in Dallas. At that time, this was one of the highest careers to which a women could aspire. Bette had become an excellent secretary and knew she would do a good job. She encountered only one hitch: mastering the newfangled electric typewriter that was provided in place of the familiar manual machine. Not to worry, she thought. She'd manage.

The first day on the job, a little hesitantly, Bette turned on the machine, began typing and brightened as she felt the keys respond to the barest touch. She was delighted. But disaster struck when she made a mistake and tried to erase it. The more she erased, the greater was the messy smudge from the film ribbon used in electric typewriters.

She retyped the letter, working more slowly and carefully, but decided then and there that no matter how competent she was, she had to be able to make corrections. The question was . . . how could she accomplish that?

Bette and her son, Michael, who would later become a pop star with The Monkees.

"I was doing some artwork for Texas Bank on a free-lance basis, trying to make a little extra money," she explained years later. "The job was helping with the design for the annual report. I knew that when artists do any lettering, they never correct by erasing. They just paint over the error. So I decided to use what they use. I put some white tempera water-based paint in a bottle, took along my watercolor brush, and used that at the office to correct my typing mistakes." It was for Bette a simple solution to a troubling problem.

For the next five years, the accuracy of her typing continued to be admired while her corrections went unnoticed. In fact, Bette was anxious that people not find out about what she called her "correction stuff" because she felt she was somehow cheating by using it.

Inevitably, other secretaries at the bank got wind of what was happening and asked her to let them have some of her secret brew. To satisfy them, Bette made her first batch of the liquid for others. The year was 1956, and Bette had just created the first of the 25 million bottles she would produce annually 19 years later.

"I used a little green bottle I found at home, wrote "MISTAKE OUT" on a file label, and stuck it on. It was my first attempt to be professional."

One day, when an office supply dealer asked her why she didn't market MISTAKE OUT, Bette thought about organizing a company. Even with both a product and a customer base, however, Bette had to overcome a

daunting series of stumbling blocks on the way to starting her new business. She needed a registered trade-
mark from the U.S. Copyright Office, but couldn't
afford the attorney's fees. So she researched how to
write the application and filed it herself. Then she
needed to obtain a patent from the U.S. Patent Office,
but that required a patent search to see if anyone else
held one on a similar product. That would cost $400—
money she couldn't afford—and since it was something
she couldn't do herself, she had no choice but to market
the product without a patent—a risky step. She also
wanted to improve the product first, because it took too
long to dry. Paying a laboratory to come up with an
improved formula was out of the question, but Bette
found a way:

"I decided I would try to work out a formula myself.
I went to the library and found the formula for a type of
tempera paint. A chemistry teacher from Michael's
school helped me a little bit, and I learned how to grind
and mix paint from a man at a paint manufacturing
company."

Using her kitchen as a lab, she spent weekends and
nights developing the wetting agent and resin that
would make the solution quick-drying as well as unde-
tectable. By 1957, she felt confident enough to ask
IBM, where she now worked as a secretary, to market
"Liquid Paper."

"I received a letter from [IBM]," said Bette some

years later, after The Gillette Company bought the Liquid Paper Corporation from her for $47.5 million, "telling me to work on improving the product a little more and then come back to them. But I decided to market the product myself and I never did go back with it to IBM."

By the end of that first year, and still working full time at her secretarial job, Bette was selling 100 bottles of Liquid Paper a month. She recruited her son, Michael, and some of his teenage friends as her first employees and she relocated her operation from the kitchen to the garage and then to a backyard portable tool shed that she purchased with a $500 loan.

In 1958, an article about Liquid Paper appeared in a national office supply magazine—the product's first national exposure. Orders flooded in from enthusiastic secretaries all across the country. The first corporate response Bette received—a request from General Electric for three gross—meant working through several nights just to fill that one order. The business was growing so much that it was starting to interfere with her full-time job as a secretary at IBM.

Bette knew at some point she would have to leave her day job, but she recalled, "I didn't have the courage to quit." As it turned out, she didn't have to quit because she was fired for making a mistake Liquid Paper couldn't correct!

"I was working all day on one job and all night on

The inventor applies a dab of Liquid Paper to a sheet in her typewriter.

my own product," she recalled. "It was hard to keep from mixing up the two. Then one day, I wrote a letter for IBM and signed it The Mistake Out Company. That did it. But getting fired was a big shock, because I depended on that job. I really had no other sure income and I had a son to provide for."

Despite the hundreds of orders she was receiving, the net profits weren't enough for her to stop completely, so Bette got another job and continued to work part time. She especially needed money to hire a chemist to perfect Liquid Paper.

In 1962, Bette married Robert Graham, a frozen food salesman. He joined her company, and she devoted herself to Liquid Paper full time. From there, its growth accelerated markedly. By 1968, when MISTAKE OUT became Liquid Paper, it was grossing more than $1 million a year, and producing 10,000 bottles a day in a brand-new manufacturing facility and office.

By 1975, the Liquid Paper Corporation had 200 employees producing and selling its product in 31 countries. It boasted an innovative form of management that included both vice presidents and secretaries, with everyone's contributions regarded equally by the corporation. It was a company now run by a woman who summed up her attitude toward business by saying to her employees, "Isn't the real value in our experience the development of our own talents? In fighting and

Bob Graham's salesmanship pushed revenues from Liquid Paper to ever-increasing levels.

winning battles?" All this had come about through the efforts of a woman who for years signed her name on correspondence as B. Nesmith, because she was afraid businessmen wouldn't take the company seriously if they knew the president was a woman!

By the time Bette died in 1980, she had established the Bette Claire McMurray Foundation and the Gihon Foundation, which have dedicated more than $2 million to the task of changing attitudes about women through research and education. The goal of these two foundations is to reflect the roles of women as artist, entrepreneur, and philosopher. McMurray Foundation grants have gone to women's and art-oriented nonprofit organizations such as the Girls Club of America, the American Film Institute, Robert Redford's Sundance Institute, The Women's Caucus for Art, the National Women's Education Fund, and The Women's Research and Education Institute.

The Gihon Foundation, named for an Old Testament river that symbolized the rights of women, is directed to educate the public about the wide range of women's art and includes among its activities a touring exhibition of art by masters such as Georgia O'Keefe,

Bottles of Liquid Paper, which now comes in many colors and has several special uses

Wealthy from the success of the product she invented, Bette Nesmith Graham contributed generously to many charitable causes.

Mary Cassatt, Grandma Moses, and Helen Frankenthaler.

Not least of Bette's many significant contributions was the formation of a company subsidiary, L.P. Child Development Corporation, which opened its first full-day child care center for working parents in late 1976. That same year, at 52, Bette resigned as chairwoman of the board of the company to become a full-time Christian Science practitioner.

When asked how she would like to be remembered, despite all she achieved as a businesswoman, this undeclared feminist and practitioner of her faith replied, "I'm an artist, an entrepreneur, and a philosopher. In my business life, I think that's true. But I think that I would really like to be known as a Christian Science Practitioner."

Bette believed in herself and described what she considered the essential element for success simply: "It is the ability to see a right idea in spite of the fact that others do not, and to cling to it in the face of discouragement and self-mistrust. As for success itself, my definition of real success is being aware that one is expressing fully and freely his or her own true individuality—his or her uniqueness, his or her innate worth."

Grace Hopper's work with computers took her to the highest ranks of the United States Navy.

110

8

Grace Hopper

*E*ven today, young women and girls are discouraged—often unconsciously—from studying mathematics. But in the 1920s, when Grace Murray Hopper was going to school, things were even worse. Still, Grace studied math, and she excelled at it. She went on to become one of America's greatest computer innovators. And she became something else very unexpected for a woman: a rear admiral in the U.S. Navy.

Hopper always credited her father with encouraging her to compete scholastically, and she and her sister received the same education as their brother. In elementary school in Wolfeboro, New Hampshire, and in high school after the family moved to New York City, Grace loved the physical sciences. Early on, teachers exposed her to geometry, and she developed an unmistakable aptitude for it. Her grades were good enough to get her into Vassar College, one of the top women's universities, where she received a degree in mathematics and physics. She earned a Phi Beta Kappa key and was awarded a fellowship, which she used to get a Masters degree and a doctorate at Yale University.

After graduation, she had to look for a job. But in 1934, five years after the stock market crashed and five years before the beginning of World War II that would revitalize the U.S. economy, the country was in the middle of the Great Depression. Men stood on bread lines—jobs for women were not only unlikely, they were irrelevant. So, when Vassar offered Dr. Hopper a teaching position at $800 a year, she jumped at the chance. It took her almost seven years to go from instructor to assistant professor to associate professor. She left with a faculty fellowship to study at New York University.

But now, the country was at war, and Dr. Hopper took a step that influenced the rest of her life. She entered the naval reserve. Why would a bright, successful associate professor from Vassar attend Midshipman's School at Northampton, Massachusetts, to emerge as a commissioned lieutenant junior grade?

"It was Navy all the way for me," explained Hopper with pride. She was a descendant of a Revolutionary War Minute Man and a Civil War captain. And there was her favorite, "the admiral": Rear Admiral Alexander Wilson Russell, her great-grandfather, who had served in the Civil War.

About this great-grandfather, Hopper said, "I was about three years old when I first met him. Although long retired, he was tall and straight, carried a black cane with a silver top on it, and had white mutton chop whiskers, which I had never seen before. He was a very impressive gentleman!"

Midshipman Hopper's orders were to the Bureau of Ordnance's computation project at Harvard University. There she would become only the third person ever to program the first large-scale computer, known as the Mark I. Today, a person can carry a computer in a shirt pocket. But the Mark I was 51 feet long, 8 feet high, and 8 feet deep! It is described today as having been "the first infant step of the computer age," able to store 72 words and perform three additions every second. A dinosaur by today's standards, many viewed it then as a mechanical miracle. And it was.

Three years later, Hopper joined the company that later became Remington Rand and then was renamed Sperry Rand. This company was building UNIVAC I, the first commercial large-scale electronic computer.

In the first days of computer development, many thought that these machines could function only by being programmed by mathematicians speaking to the computer in precise numerical language. Everything had to be translated into a function of "0" and "1," a very arcane and time-consuming way of communicating. But in 1952, Grace Murray Hopper came up with a concept that allowed programmers to instruct a computer in, if not English, at least an English-like language. She developed a device that would make a computer understand commands like "add," "execute," and "stop." Hopper called her device the computer compiler. Her discovery was essentially that starting from scratch every time a person writes a program is inefficient. So, she said, let's write a basic program that gives every computer a basic understanding of its function, like how to take orders. Then, more sophisticated programmers can come in and give those orders. The "compiler" would be a sort of translator. Critics said, "It can't be done." Hopper replied, "It can so!"

Hopper and her staff did, indeed, demonstrate a working model of the computer compiler. Ultimately, it led to the development of a widely used computer language called COBOL, short for COmmon Business Oriented Languages. For the first time, a computer user could tell the machine to "quit" instead of to "01100110101100101001100011 . . ." and on and on.

Hopper's next project had to do with reducing the time and effort UNIVAC I spent solving numerical scientific problems. She put together a manual detailing some of her earlier work, called Flow-Matic Programming. By now, her work in computers was

Captain Hopper spent much of her 43-year naval career working on computer programming language.

leaving the ultrahigh security world of the U.S. Navy and starting to revolutionize the business world.

Hopper often found that getting her ideas across was as much a struggle as coming up with them. On more than one occasion, she experienced what she described as the "dreadful frustration of trying to push innovative ideas into the future." She had to weather the criticisms of admirals and generals, budget directors, and business executives—"all resolutely united by a stubborn resistance to change."

But Hopper understood the inevitability of change. When she was born in 1906, the world in general considered the automobile and the airplane to be mechanical "gadgets." No refrigerators or radios existed. The first transcontinental telephone call, from New York to San Francisco, had yet to be made. She lived to see men walk on the moon, to see busy workers send messages by a fax machine, to see preschoolers operate computers.

Later in her life, one of Admiral Hopper's trademarks was a clock she kept on her office wall. Its hands ran backwards, counterclockwise. It was a visual reminder, she said, that just because something has always been done a certain way doesn't mean that's the only way to do it. Grace Murray Hopper's least favorite answer was "But we've always done it that way before."

When Hopper became Director of Programming Languages in the Office of the Chief of Naval Operations, her job was to standardize high-level computer languages for the navy. Developing user-friendly computer programming languages became her specialty, and this revolutionized computer software. Almost as important was her approach to data management. Data, she explained, is simply raw material. With the proper use of computers, data can become useful information.

When World War II was over, Hopper joined the faculty of Harvard University as a research fellow in engineering sciences and applied physics. She worked at the computation laboratories on continued successors to the Mark I. By then, she was 40 years old and a

Grace Hopper, the first woman to be called back to active duty, works at her desk in the office of the Chief of Naval Operations.

lieutenant in the naval reserve. When she asked to be made regular navy, they told her she was too old. Twenty years later, in 1966, Hopper retired from the naval reserve. A year later, the navy recalled her to active duty and almost immediately promoted her to captain. Too old, indeed!

Hopper recognized early on how great the applications of computers could be. To spread the message, she wrote more than 50 articles and taught at five different universities. Industry veterans agree that one of her greatest contributions was her ability to attract the interest of businesses, such as insurance companies and the aerospace industry. She also helped bridge the gap between management and the programmers. This plain-speaking Yankee could talk to management in terms it understood! Hopper explained her success by saying, "With any new idea, you have to sell that idea and market it. In the long run, you don't do it by logic. You've got to show that guy why it's in his interest to accept a new way."

Hopper was more than author, scientist, researcher, educator, and naval officer. She was also a world traveler who covered more than 100,000 miles a year here and abroad, lecturing about computers. She was well rewarded and recognized in her work: When Sweden invited her to receive an honorary doctorate in engineering from Linkoping University, she dined with the Swedish king and queen. When Bucknell University awarded her an honorary doctorate, the college president wrote, "Your pioneering contributions to the development of computer systems and computer programming have won for you an international reputation and the respect of all who honor excellence."

Throughout her life, Hopper remained an advocate of continuing computer use. Right before her 80th birthday—when she retired!—an interviewer asked her

In September 1985, Commodore Hopper spoke during the groundbreaking ceremony for the Grace M. Hopper Navy Regional Data Automation Center at the North Island, California, Naval Air Station.

whether a paper-free environment was possible. Grace replied, "We're putting on paper a lot of stuff that never needed to be on paper. We do need to keep the records, but there isn't any reason for printing them. The next generation growing up with computers will change that. Magazines, newspapers and books—those we'll keep. But not all this junk we pile up."

Everywhere she looked, Hopper saw new applications for computers. "The population of the world is increasing, as is the need to increase the world's food supply," she stated. "Long-range weather forecasts provided by computers," she said, "will help facilitate plans for planting crops. Water allocations will also prove to be a major computer effort." She also said the following:

"NASA uses a computer to scan data to see if the color of the desert changes. If the color changes, there might be oil under it.

"We could use computers to track locusts that are attacking a crop.

"I know of a fisherman who uses his computer to keep track of the fish in his lake.. Every time he catches a fish, he notes in his file what part of the lake, what time of day, what the weather was, what lure he used, what kind of fish, how heavy it was. That's storing information and making it directly accessible."

Hopper believed that computers could even revolutionize medicine. "There's a system for identifying

In 1987, Rear Admiral Grace Hopper, USN Retired, received an honorary doctor of letters degree from Drexel University President William S. Gaither.

infections called MYCIN. Experts have collected information from doctors all over the United States. When a doctor calls in with specific infection symptoms, the system comes back and asks him if he's noticed this or noticed that. The doctor answers. The system says, 'I think you're treating such and such, and you should do this.' It's something we couldn't have imagined a few years ago."

Hopper, however, never felt that the world had begun to depend too much on computers. "Either you use computers or you can't do the job," she said. "It's just gotten too big. Look at banking. They couldn't compute all those things for all those individuals and for all those individual services if you didn't have the computers. You have revolving credit accounts in stores. You couldn't have any of that stuff without the computer. All that personalized service depends on the computer."

To the question of whether there is a limit to what computers can do for us, Hopper's responded, "They'll only be limited if our imaginations are limited. It's all up to us. Remember, there were people who said the airplane couldn't fly."

When finally, at age 79, Rear Admiral Grace Murray Hopper was obliged to retire from the U.S. Navy, she promptly signed on as full-time senior consultant at Digital Equipment Corporation, a manufacturer of minicomputers in Washington, D.C. In that position, she represented the company at forums and meetings and in the company's relations with educational institutions.

When Grace Hopper died in 1992, the 37 honorary degrees and 30 professional awards listed in her obituary tesfified both to her remarkable naval service and to her career as a gifted mathematician who made use of her talents to expand the horizons of the computer.

Barbara and Ken, models for the most popular dolls in history, smile with their parents, Ruth and Elliot Handler.

9

Ruth Handler

*T*he Barbie doll is the biggest success story in the toy industry. Every year, people around the world spend as much money on Barbie dolls, Barbie clothes, and Barbie accessories as they do on record albums or even movie tickets. Yet when Ruth Handler first proposed the idea of a grown-up doll to the toy designers at Mattel—the company she and her husband ran—the designers thought she was crazy. Little girls want to pretend to be mommies, she was told.

No, said Handler. Little girls want to pretend to be *bigger* girls. And she knew this because she spent a lot of time observing one little girl in particular—her daughter, Barbara, nicknamed "Barbie."

"She always played with her paper dolls, grown-up dolls with fashionable outfits," said Handler. "I thought we should make a doll like those paper dolls, but three-dimensional. A doll with breasts and a narrow waist and painted fingernails. When I told my people what I wanted to do, they looked at me like I was asking the impossible."

But Ruth Handler is like the marines: The improbable she does right away; the impossible just takes a little longer! All her life, Ruth has considered the word *no* just another challenge.

When Ruth graduated from East Denver High School and announced her intention to attend college, her family didn't give her a lot of encouragement. Marrying her high-school sweetheart—a broke-but-talented artist named Elliot Handler—was more traditional than going to university. But she ended up at the University of Denver. And she married Elliot anyway!

When she took two semesters of business education at the University of California at Los Angeles, she was the only married woman in her class. And she became the first woman to complete the program!

Ruth fell in love with Southern California. One day, she happened to visit a friend at the Paramount Studios lot in Hollywood. What she saw thrilled her—actors and actresses, working crews, lively activity all around. The place was a young girl's dream come true.

"How do I get a job here?" she asked.

"Impossible," was the reply.

"Where do you go to apply?" she persisted.

"Forget it," advised her friend.

But that wasn't Ruth's style. She was unlikely to forget anything she wanted badly. So she applied. The same day, the studio hired her as a stenographer.

The year was 1937. Ruth worked at Paramount until 1941, when she became pregnant with Barbara. The only time in her adult life that Ruth didn't work was between 1941 and 1944, when she had her son, Ken. Staying home made Ruth restless; she wanted to help Elliot run his giftware and costume jewelry business. "You make something; I'll sell it," she told him.

In 1944, while the United States was embroiled in World War II, Elliot designed a new style of picture frame made out of the then-revolutionary new plastics like Lucite. His partner, Harold "Matt" Matson, built samples and Ruth took the frames to a chain of photography studios and got a large order. The three celebrated, calling their new business "Mattel," after MATT and ELliot.

"The very next day, [as I was] driving home in the car, the president of the United States got on the radio and issued an edict," remembers Ruth. "There would be no further use of plastic for civilian use. Not even scrap. The three of us gathered that night: 'What do we do?'"

Fortunately, Elliot came up with an idea: "We can make frames out of scrap wood." Ruth took the new samples back to the photography studio and got an even bigger order. Mattel could continue operating. The leftover wood from the picture frames led to a thriving business making doll house furniture. That led to one of the most successful companies in the toy industry.

Mattel developed one innovative toy after another: a plastic ukulele, a piano with raised black keys, an affordable crank-operated music box, and much more. The company was doing well, but two significant developments changed it from a highly profitable business to a corporate giant.

The first development occurred when Mattel decided to make use of an exciting new medium called television. The company went on the air, sponsoring Walt Disney's new "Mickey Mouse Club" show. For the first time, instead of selling exclusively through factory representatives, jobbers, wholesalers, and retailers, a toy company was selling directly to its customers. From a sales volume of $5 million, Mattel went to $14 million in three years. And then came Barbie, first thought up by Ruth in 1956 and finally brought to market in 1959.

Ruth didn't sculpt Barbie or sew the dresses. Engineers and technicians hold the patents on the doll itself. And Ruth hired a fashion designer named Charlotte Johnson to create Barbie's wardrobe. "I set down the specifications and approved every single thing," Handler explains, "but the physical work was done by others. The important thing about design is to know what you want, what the characteristics of the final product should be. Then you get technicians to make it happen."

Getting Barbie ready for the 1959 New York Toy Show was every bit as traumatic as a coming-out party for a society debutante! When the show opened, the buyers were less than enthusiastic, but the public decided differently. The response was tremendous!

The original BARBIE® doll, 1959

Throughout the country and worldwide, Mattel sold millions of Ruth Handler's Barbie dolls, boosting the company's sales to $18 million. Within ten years, customers bought $500 million worth of Barbie products.

As co-founder of Mattel with her husband, Elliot, Ruth moved up the company's chain of command from executive vice president to president to co-chairman of the board of directors. These titles were practically unheard of for women in the 1960s.

Handler remembers one episode that occurred to her in the business world despite her executive status. A brokerage house was holding a meeting with the investment community at a private club, and Handler was to be the keynote speaker for the event. When she arrived at the club, she couldn't figure out why the program planners were escorting her into the club through the alley and kitchen. Later, she discovered that she was being sneaked into the building because the club rules didn't allow women!

Over the years, Handler would hold prestigious offices such as a director of the Federal Reserve Bank of San Francisco, member of the National Business Council for Consumer Affairs, and guest professor at UCLA and USC.

Then in 1970, life suddenly changed for Ruth Handler. Diagnosed with breast cancer, she immediately underwent a radical mastectomy of the left breast. The surgery left her, in her words, "unwomanized and disfigured." This happened at a time when the company was having financial problems. Badly depressed, she retired from the business.

"I had lost my self-confidence," she explained, "because I had lost my self-esteem after the mastectomy. You can't be an executive if you can't lead with confidence. I couldn't stop crying, and I couldn't get rid of the hostility. I had always been able to manage my life very well. This I couldn't manage."

Ruth Handler's company, Mattel, successfully markets KEN®, BARBIE®, and related toys throughout the world.

Although severe, the depression didn't last long. In typical fashion, Ruth began to seek solutions to the problem. She looked for a prosthesis to substitute for her missing breast. The market offered many, but she didn't like any of them. More specifically, she hated them! "They were egg-shaped globs, heavy and shapeless and not at all matching the other breast when worn in a brassiere."

She went into action. First, she persuaded a prosthesis designer named Peyton Massey to make her an artificial breast according to her specifications. "I walked in and said, 'Peyton, I'm going to make commercial breasts available to everybody, with separate rights and lefts that contour to the body, and in bra sizes.' He said I was crazy, but I convinced him to help me."

Next door to Massey's office was an old storage room. In this room, Handler, Massey, and the newly hired staff, set up shop. Ruth did the running around to assemble the lab equipment they needed. To help her learn about the manufacturing process and most appropriate materials to use, she located three retired Mattel workers and she enlisted Elliot, who was also now retired from Mattel. Thus began the company she named "Nearly Me."

The new product from Nearly Me was a contoured and tapered breast design made of polyurethane outer skin over silicone gel in the front and foam at the back.

Most importantly, the device gave structure and shape to match the true breast exactly. A woman in need of the prosthesis could order it in a regular brassiere size and wear it with a regular bra.

Almost a year later, Ruth moved from the little storage area to a factory and office in West Los Angeles. The Nearly Me company went on to introduce bathing suits and other products needed by mastectomies. In the meantime, Ruth lost her other breast to cancer. But Nearly Me gave her something to work toward—helping other women survive what she had gone through. Most company personnel trained in fitting Nearly Me products on customers were themselves mastectomies.

After 16 years of overseeing every facet of the company, Ruth sold Nearly Me in 1991 to Spenco, a subsidiary of Kimberly Clark.

"I never went into the business to make money, although Nearly Me has been successful," she explains. "The idea was to help women just like myself who needed all of the self-esteem they could get after radical surgery."

Ruth Handler did, however, become a wealthy woman from her inventions. In her 70s, living in comfortable retirement at the beach, she plays bridge at the country club, keeps an office in a Century City highrise, and continues to do some consulting work. "It's hard to learn to retire," she smiles. "I've led a very, very busy life."

A recent photograph of Ruth Handler

Indeed, a visitor can tell this by the awards that litter Handler's desk: Outstanding Business Woman Award, National Association of Accountants, 1961; Couple of the Year Award, Los Angeles City Council, 1963; American Marketing Association Outstanding Marketing Achievement Team Award, 1964; *Los Angeles Times* Woman of the Year in Business, 1968;

Brotherhood Award, National Conference of Christian and Jews, 1972.

"I observed the need, I observed the void in the market. And I defined the characteristics of the product that would fill it." And from that, her children have been forever immortalized: Barbie and Ken, best friends to three generations.

This is how BARBIE® has looked during four decades, including models (left to right) from 1989, 1977, 1968, and 1959.

Working as a scientist at DuPont, Stephanie Kwolek developed the ultra-strong fiber known as Kevlar.

10

Stephanie Kwolek

*P*erhaps some of the police officers who wear bullet-resistant vests know that the material in them is Kevlar, a fiber five times stronger than steel. And maybe some of the people who drive steel-belted radial tires know that the "steel" is often not metal at all, but Kevlar aramid synthetic fiber. The scientists who put Kevlar in space vehicles may even know that a chemist at DuPont invented this amazing fiber, and that the patents are in the name of "S.L. Kwolek." But do any of them know that "S.L." stands for "Stephanie Louise"?

Stephanie Louise Kwolek has spent her career at the DuPont Company, working, as she calls it, as a "bench chemist." She holds 28 different patents in her speciality, which is low-temperature polymerization—in other words, making ultra-resilient synthetics under special laboratory conditions. She discovered the first liquid crystal polymers, which created an entire branch of research and invention. Her 1971 patent for Kevlar revolutionized the synthetics industry and made millions for DuPont. It has also saved thousands of lives.

Of course, when Stephanie Kwolek first came to DuPont—then known as the E. I. DuPont de Nemours Company—no one expected her to invent one of the company's most coveted products. They didn't much want a woman in the research lab in the first place and certainly didn't expect one to stay for 40 years.

"This wasn't the career I planned," said Kwolek, shortly before her retirement in 1986.

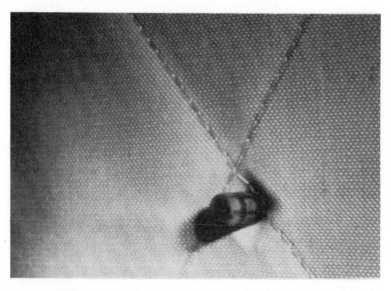

Special film shows a bullet hitting but not penetrating this vest made of Kevlar.

I wanted to study medicine. But when I left college, I didn't have enough money for med school. I thought I would work for a while, and save up some money. When I joined DuPont in 1946, women were having a very difficult time in science. Women who got jobs in the lab would stay only a few years; they were encouraged to move into so-called "women's fields." They were not promoted as rapidly as the men—women I know, even Ph.D. women, lasted about two or three years, and then went back to teaching, frequently at a women's college. But there were some of us who decided to stick it out, and I was one. The work was so interesting. I was right there at the beginning when low-temperature polymerization was discovered. Right there to make the discoveries. I've had a very exciting and gratifying career.

Stephanie Louise was born in New Kensington, Pennsylvania, on July 31, 1923, to John and Nellie Zajdel Kwolek. Her dad worked as a mold-maker in the local foundry. She grew up a curious, independent child, the kind who catches frogs and turns over rocks to see what's underneath.

"My father was a naturalist by avocation," Kwolek recalled in 1992. "I remember spending an awful lot of time with my father, roaming through the woods, collecting wildflowers and seeds and making scrapbooks of them."

Little Stephanie knew exactly what she wanted to be: a scientist. Well, either a scientist or a fashion designer. She created elaborate paper outfits for her paper dolls, and learned to sew. "When I was six, I loved to use my mother's sewing machine. I was forbidden to use the sewing machine, but I would sneak in when my mother went shopping."

Everything changed when Stephanie was ten. Her father died, and her mother went to work for the Aluminum Company of America to support Stephanie and her brother. So even during the 1930s, Stephanie was used to the idea of a working woman. Her mother encouraged her to go to college, and in 1942 Stephanie enrolled at nearby Carnegie-Mellon University.

World War II was a scary, exciting time to be going to college. Science was at the forefront; new discoveries, from radar to the atomic bomb, were on everyone's lips. Because the men were overseas fighting, jobs were opening up to women as they never had before. Stephanie majored in chemistry, took lots of biology, and graduated with a Bachelor of Science degree.

When she joined the DuPont Company of Wilmington, Delaware, Kwolek was thrown right into some of the fastest growing areas of industrial scientific research. Synthetic fabrics were first discovered and marketed during the war. Nylon was first produced in 1939, making silk stockings all but obsolete. (When nylon stockings went on the market in 1940, women stood in line overnight outside their local hosiery shops, so they could be the first to own a pair.)

Chemists all over the country were finding new ways

to spin fibers from petrochemical compounds. DuPont scientists discovered Dacron polyester, Orlon acrylic, and Lycra spandex, all of which are still in use 50 years later.

Kwolek's job was working on aromatic polymers. "Polymer" means the chemical has a long molecular chain. "Aromatic" means one of the molecules is something called a benzene ring. Benzene rings attach to each other like Tinkertoys, stretching out into long chains of molecules. If a scientist hit on the right solution (liquid mixture) of aromatic polymer, she or he might be able to spin it into a fiber of unusual strength and resilience. That's what Kwolek was trying to do.

Throughout the 1950s, Kwolek continued her work. Most chemists were working on polymers that dissolved at very high temperatures, and they spun these into fiber. Kwolek was looking for polymers that could be dissolved at less than the boiling point of water—polymers that could be spun even at room temperature. Low-temperature polymerization became her specialty.

Kwolek later related how she made her groundbreaking discovery: "Then, in 1964, I was assigned to find new high-performance polymers. Stable at high temperature, stable to acids, stable to bases." DuPont was looking for material as indestructible as the fabric in Superman's suit. Kwolek began looking at polymer solutions called *liquid crystals*. Unlike the molecules in most solutions, all the molecules in liquid crystals line up in a single direction. Under a microscope, most polymers look like cooked spaghetti, random and twisty and splurged together. However, liquid crystal polymers look like raw spaghetti, neatly lined up in a row.

"Every step was a challenge," said Kwolek. She had to come up with new solvents to create her solution, new ways to achieve the desired result. She spent a month making different combinations and finally developed a solution that acted like nothing she had ever seen. All the other polymer solutions were transparent and viscous, like melted glass. This polymer turned opalescent (pearl-like) when she stirred it, and it had the texture of buttermilk. The lab assistant didn't even want to put it in the spinneret.

Kwolek remembered that "after much coaxing, I convinced the technician to spin the solution. And the fiber that resulted was not only very strong, it was very stiff. Stiffer than glass fiber. We had it tested for strength and stiffness, and when the properties came back, I was amazed they were so high." Kwolek's new fiber had incredible strength.

"I had the results repeated a number of times before I told anyone," she said. "They were so unusual, I didn't want to be embarrassed if they were incorrect!"

Kwolek patented the process for making this unique fiber, named Kevlar. She assigned the patent to DuPont, but received both a generous bonus and a long overdue promotion for her discovery.

Kwolek displays Kevlar in liquid form.

Flames swirl around a pair of gloves made of Kevlar, but they do not burn.

Stephanie and her lab team continued to study Kevlar. They discovered it was lighter than asbestos and stronger than steel (and would not rust). It could be made into yarn, pulp, paper, pellets, and thread. It could be used in everything from body armor to aircraft parts to uniforms to circuit boards. Today it's made into inflatable boats, sail cloth, parachutes, even building materials. Woodcutters use Kevlar gloves to keep from chopping their fingers off, and oil-riggers use Kevlar ropes to keep floating oil platforms attached to the ocean bottom.

Kevlar has even saved lives. DuPont recently estimated that in 20 years of using Kevlar in bullet-resistant vests, the lives of 1,300 law enforcement officers have been saved.

Kwolek has received many awards for her inventions and discoveries. She was given the American Society of Metals Award in 1978 and both the American Chemical Society Creative Invention Award and the American Institute of Chemists Chemical Pioneer Award in 1980. Worcester Polytechnic Institute in Massachusetts honored her with a Doctor of Science degree in 1981, for "contributions to polymer and fiber chemistry," and the Polymer Processing Hall of Fame welcomed her as a member in 1985.

In 1991, Kwolek was nominated to be the first woman inducted into the Inventors Hall of Fame. (Although she wasn't accepted, one woman, Gertrude Elion, Nobel Prize winner in medicine, did become a member. Elion developed drugs to treat leukemia, herpes, gout, and organ transplant rejection.)

Stephanie lives in Delaware in the home she bought in 1977. As a retirement gift for herself, she went out and bought herself the fanciest, most expensive sewing machine on the market but has hardly had a minute to

Rolls of Kevlar in a DuPont factory

use it since. Instead, she consults for DuPont and the National Research Council of the National Academy of Sciences and she goes around the country—indeed, the world—speaking to other researchers and to students about her specialty. She likes to garden and read (especially biography), and, of course, she designs and sews her own clothes.

"I love going to schools to demonstrate chemistry to children," she has said. Getting young people interested in science thrills her because people have odd images of what a woman scientist should be like. This particular woman scientist looks a lot like a leprechaun: not even five feet tall, gray hair cut in pudding-bowl style, an amused dimple.

Although she never married, Kwolek was once engaged. But she was transferred by her firm, and the long-distance relationship didn't work out. For 40 years, she has essentially been married to the lab, and most of the time, that "marriage" has been a good relationship.

"Happiness isn't the result of being with someone else," she says, "although that is nice. I never thought in my life that my only objective was to be happy. I think my objective was to be productive—and along the way, being productive has made me happy."

Bibliography

Baker, Sara Josephine. *Fighting For Life*. New York: Robert E. Krieger, 1980.

Barron, Janet J. "Prioritizing Information." *Byte*, May 1991. (Interview with Grace Murray Hopper)

Betts, Mitch. "Grace Murray Hopper, Mother of COBOL." *Computerworld*, 6 January 1992.

Coston, Martha. *A Signal Success: The Work and Travels of Mrs. Martha J. Coston*. Philadelphia: J.B. Lippincott, 1886.

Cunningham, Marian, ed. *The Fannie Farmer Cookbook*. 12th ed. New York: Knopf, 1992.

Hamblen, Diane. "Only the Limits of Our Imagination: An Exclusive Interview with RADM Grace M. Hopper." *Chips Ahoy*, July 1986.

Johnson, Steve. "Grace Hopper—A Living Legend." *All Hands*, September 1982.

Keller, Evelyn Fox. *A Feeling for the Organism: The Life and Work of Barbara McClintock.* San Francisco: W.H. Freeman, 1983.

Leopold, George. "Beacon for the Future." *Datamation*, 1 October 1992. (Interview with Grace Murray Hopper)

McClintock, Barbara. *The Discovery of Characterization of Transposable Elements: The Collected Papers of Barbara McClintock.* New York: Garland Papers, 1987.

Pinckney, Eliza Lucas. *The Letterbox of Eliza Lucas Pinckney, 1739-1762.* Edited by Elise Pinckney with Marvin R. Zahniser. Chapel Hill: University of North Carolina Press, 1972.

Steele, Zuma. "Fannie Farmer and Her Cook Book." *American Mercury*, July 1944.

Vare, Ethlie, and Greg Ptacek. *Mothers of Invention.* New York: William Morrow, 1988.

The authors also wish to acknowledge information received from the Bette Claire McMurray Foundation, Dallas, Texas; Madam C. J. Walker Urban Life Center, Indianapolis, Indiana; Walker Manufacturing, Tuskegee, Alabama; as well as personal interviews with Ruth Handler, Los Angeles, California, and Stephanie Kwolek, Wilmington, Delaware.

Index

Photo Credits

ABOUT THE AUTHORS

ETHLIE ANN VARE became fascinated with women inventors when writing the award-winning *Mothers of Invention: From the Bra to the Bomb, Forgotten Women and Their Unforgettable Ideas.* She has also written biographies of rock stars Stevie Nicks and Ozzy Osbourne, actors Harrison Ford and Martin Sheen, and scientist Ellen Swallow Richards. She reports on the Hollywood scene for magazines in England, Australia, and New Zealand. Vare is originally from Montreal, Canada. She is a graduate of the University of Calfornia at Santa Barbara and lives in Los Angeles with her son, Russell, and her dog, Troila.

GREG PTACEK is the co-author of *Mothers of Invention: From the Bra to the Bomb, Forgotten Women and Their Unforgettable Ideas.* Currently a marketing executive for an independent film company, Ptacek is developing *Mothers of Invention* into a television documentary special. He is also co-author of *The 150 Best Companies for Liberal Arts Graduates.* A former journalist specializing in the entertainment industry, he served as a film reporter for the daily entertainment newspaper, *The Hollywood Reporter.* Originally from Virginia, Ptacek is a graduate of Tulane Universtiy and of the University of Southern California. He currently resides in Los Angeles.